WESTMAR COLLE

PRAEGER PATHFINDER BIOGRAPHIES

SAMUEL GOMPERS: *Leader of American Labor*
by Will Chasan

MARTIN LUTHER: *Leader of the Reformation*
by Leonard W. Cowie

ARISTOTLE: *Founder of Scientific Philosophy*
by Benjamin Farrington

FRANCIS BACON: *Pioneer of Planned Science*
by Benjamin Farrington

MADAME CURIE: *Pioneer of the Atomic Age*
by Alan Ivimey

HILDAGO: *Mexican Revolutionary*
by Mark Lieberman

SIGMUND FREUD: *Founder of Psychoanalysis*
by Agnes M. McGlashan and
Christopher J. Reeve

CHARLES DARWIN: *Pioneer in the Theory of Evolution*
by H. E. L. Mellersh

MOHAMMED: *Prophet of the Religion of Islam*
by E. Royston Pike

Juárez of Mexico

W. Wendell Blancké

PRAEGER PUBLISHERS
New York • Washington • London

PRAEGER PUBLISHERS
111 Fourth Avenue, New York, N.Y. 10003, U.S.A.
5, Cromwell Place, London SW7 2JL, England

Published in the United States of America in 1971
by Praeger Publishers, Inc.

Library of Congress Catalog Card Number: 75–143964

Printed in the United States of America

Contents

6 Contents

List of Illustrations

7

Juárez of Mexico

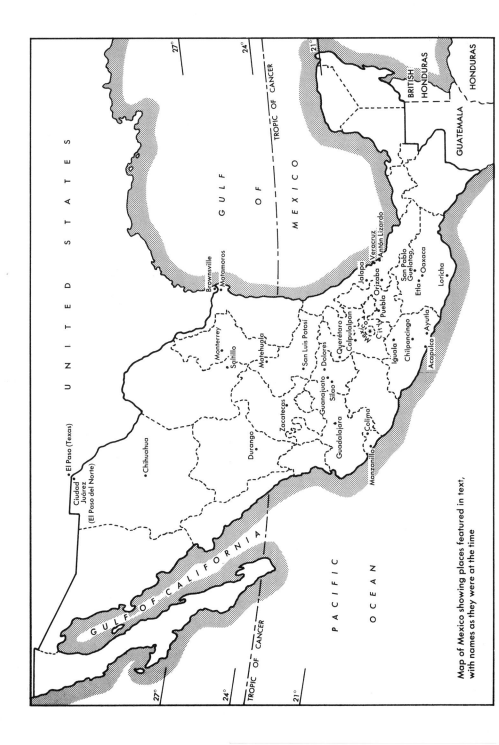

Map of Mexico showing places featured in text, with names as they were at the time

1

Prologue

THE YEAR is 1858, in the first days of what is to be a long and bitter civil war. The new President of Mexico and his government are on the run. Fleeing the capital, they have reached the loyal city of Guadalajara, in the west. No sooner have they set up headquarters in the Statehouse, than they learn that their main army has been disastrously defeated nearby.

News of the rout is already about town. As the President and his cabinet confer on defense of the city with the General commanding the area, the Governor hurries in with another report. The palace guard has mutinied and is marching on the Statehouse.

The President sends the General out to see what is going on. Before long, all hell breaks loose. With shouts of "Long live religion!" the mutinous guards break in, seize the President and his staff, and herd them into a large room. Outside, there is chaos. Troops loyal to the President are already gathering to occupy adjacent buildings. The mutineers have opened a nearby jail and have pressed the convicts into service, under command of "a priest of ferocious appearance."

The General who was sent to reconnoiter is brought back under guard and thrown in with the rest of the President's

party. He shows them the pieces of his vest-pocket watch. It
has just deflected a bullet aimed at his chest.

The troops loyal to the President keep up a running fire from
adjoining buildings. That night, a mutineer officer comes to the
President with a demand that he call off the siege. The
President, a stocky, dark-skinned Indian dressed in sober black
broadcloth, replies with cool dignity that, as a prisoner, he is in
no position to issue orders. The mutineer departs. The party
spends a cold, hungry night.

Next morning, after discussion with his cabinet, the
President consents to a truce. Bugles sound. A parley is set up.
Intermediaries meet in a nearby convent.

Not all the loyal forces, however, have been kept informed of
developments. One officer, unaware of the truce, moves in to
launch a surprise attack on the Statehouse in an attempt to
rescue his chief. The assault is repulsed but the mutineers are
furious. They believe they have been betrayed under the guise
of truce and turn upon the hostages.

A voice cries out: "They are coming to kill us!" The
President, poker-faced, advances to the door. Mutineer soldiers
enter the room, take aim, and await the command to fire. Benito
Juárez° flings back his head, his bright black eyes full upon the
leveled muskets, and waits impassively.

°Approximate Mexican pronunciation of Juárez: HWAH-race.

2

The Mexico of Young Benito

WHAT MANNER of man was this Benito Juárez, this full-blooded Zapotec Indian who rose from the humblest of peasant beginnings and labored with unswerving determination—against great odds and, often, at grave peril—to win his country's fight for true independence and to lay the foundations of the authentic nationhood Mexico enjoys today? Let us begin his story with a look at the Mexico in which he grew up.

At the turn of the nineteenth century, the Viceroy of His Most Catholic Majesty in New Spain had his base in Mexico City. He ruled over a great part of the North American continent, from Guatemala to Vancouver Island and from Florida to San Francisco. In addition to the whole of modern Mexico, his dominions included the territory now comprising the states of Washington, Oregon, California, Idaho, Nevada, Utah, Arizona, New Mexico, Texas, Florida, Montana, Wyoming, Colorado, North and South Dakota, Nebraska, Kansas, Oklahoma, Minnesota, Iowa, Missouri, Arkansas, and Louisiana. In 1800, Napoleon Bonaparte talked the weak-willed King of Spain into ceding back to France—in exchange for military support in Europe—the large "Louisiana" region that Spain had gained from France during the Seven Years' War (1756–63). Napoleon, however, soon found it expedient to

unload the territory and made a deal with the United States—
the Louisiana Purchase of 1803. The American Government,
thus, took over all but the first ten of the states named above and
a part of Colorado.

Nevertheless, when Benito Juárez was born in 1806, the
Spanish Viceroy's domain was still a large and noble
proconsulate. The German scientist Alexander von Humboldt
estimated that, in 1808, there were some 6 million people in
the Viceroy's Mexico: 2 to 3 million pure-blooded Indians, a
like number of mestizos (mixed Spanish and Indian), and the
rest ethnic Spanish—including both those born in Spain and the
Creoles, those born in Mexico of Spanish parents. Another
source estimates that those born in Spain numbered less than
50,000.

The power of the small Spanish-born oligarchy rested on a
twofold foundation. Its principal base was a feudal system of
lords and serfs. The ruling class comprised a landed aristocracy,
a military caste, and a church that was a state within a state—
immune from the law of the land, owning over half the wealth
and absolute in matters of religion and education. The peasants
were bound to the land: the Indians were sullen but submissive;
the mestizos' rising aspirations were frustrated by the system.

The secondary base of Spanish power lay in the colonial
system of monopoly for the European-born. This set white
against white, son against father. Children born in the New
World were debarred from enjoyment of the political rights of
those born in Spain. They tended, therefore, to look upon their
fathers as masters and oppressors.

On the economic side, the monopolistic system went so far as
to prohibit the colonies from raising or manufacturing any
article produced or manufactured in the mother country. (A
vestigial side-effect of this mania for monopoly may be seen in
the narrow streets and sidewalks that, even today, cause
problems in many a Latin American "inner city." Inhabitants
put the blame on Spain, which they say would not tolerate any

colonial construction that dared to improve on the Spanish way.)

Although their inferiority was largely fictitious, the Creoles were restless. The North American colonies had won their independence, and the French had violently overthrown their monarch. Throughout the New World, from Argentina to Mexico, the independence contagion was spreading, and the winds of change were felt. By the time Juárez was eighteen years old and a student at Oaxaca° Seminary, Mexico had thrown off Spanish rule in three convulsive waves, had endured a year of domestic monarchy, and had proclaimed itself a republic. Let us turn our attention briefly to these five important chapters of Mexican history.

1810

The first independence wave was a premature uprising of the masses sparked and led by the visionary and volatile patriot-priest Miguel Hidalgo. On September 16, 1810, at daybreak, a wild ringing of bells summoned the townsfolk to church in the village of Dolores, near Mexico City. Rumors were already in the air, and the church filled rapidly. As soon as he had a capacity crowd, Padre Hidalgo mounted the pulpit and gave out a thundering *"Mexicanos, viva México!"* This has since been regarded as Mexico's proclamation of independence. On every September 16, the President, in Mexico City, and the state governors, in their capitals, appear on their balconies and give Hidalgo's famous cry, the *"Grito de Dolores."* They are answered by roared *viva*'s from the crowd below. The national anthem is played with spirit. There are fireworks and rejoicing.

Hidalgo was, above all, a champion of the underdog. Aside from his lieutenants and a small band of Creole intellectuals, it was the underdog masses who followed him. He promised not

°Approximate Mexican pronunciation of Oaxaca: Wah-HAH-kah.

only an end to Spanish rule but also racial equality, redistribution of the land, and equal justice for all. His crusade started out as a movement for independence, which was one thing. It soon became a social and economic war of the have-nots against the haves, which was something else again. The Creole establishment, alarmed, was driven onto the side of the unloved Spaniards.

Hidalgo's undisciplined mob of Indians and mestizos, armed with "shotguns, spears, and clubs," overran much of the Mexican countryside but never really had a chance. By March of 1811, his forces had been definitively beaten and he and his lieutenants captured. Soon thereafter, he was given a summary court-martial, defrocked by the Inquisition, and turned over to the army to be shot.

The pioneer of independence could not ride the storm he had called into being. Still, the brief, glorious six months of his ascendancy were enough to shake the whole social structure of New Spain. Padre Hidalgo was a true forerunner of revolution. He advanced his cause against insuperable odds by courage, example, and sacrifice. His enterprise was doomed from the beginning to disaster, but by no means to extinction.

1811–15

Although Hidalgo's head was put in an iron cage and hung up as a warning to other possible troublemakers, that warning went unheeded in one important quarter. The banner of revolt was caught up by another hero-priest, José María Morelos. Endowed with social vision equal to that of Hidalgo, Morelos was gifted, as well, with military talents and organizing ability that the pioneer had lacked. The second surge also fell short, but it lasted four years and came within sight of the goal. Morelos held the royalist forces in play and harassed them in their strongholds. He managed to threaten and, at times, cut off trade routes to the capital. Instead of a chaotic mass uprising, he produced an organized insurrection. Morelos was aided in no small part by the early support of several influential Creole clans. These allies rallied to his banner, complete with private peasant armies from their estates. More than just a band of guerrillas, less than an army, Morelos' militia was flexible, tenacious, and effective. It gave the King's men more than one bloody nose.

Not the least of Morelos' exploits was his capture of the city of Oaxaca, which he held for more than a year. Memories of this stirring period must have been vivid in 1818, when the twelve-year-old Benito Juárez left his village and walked to Oaxaca to seek his fortune.

In late 1813, Morelos overreached himself and met a disastrous defeat; that marked the beginning of his end. Before this happened, however, he managed to convoke a congress of partisans to draft a constitution. This democratic document proclaimed as cardinal principles the abolition of class distinctions and of class privileges and immunities of every kind—including those of the military and the clergy. It called for separation of church and state. It also sketched out an "antipoverty program," providing rates of pay and means of subsistence for the exploited peasantry.

In 1815, this second great priest-revolutionary was caught, condemned, and defrocked. So great was Morelos' popularity that the military was ordered to shoot him without fanfare, in a small town well removed from the capital.

1821

The third, successful movement of 1821 was, in reality, a betrayal as far as the Mexican masses were concerned. It nullified the democratic, egalitarian inspiration of the first two waves by permitting a Creole aristocracy, through maneuver and intrigue, simply to supplant the Spanish.

In Spain, itself, the political pendulum had been swinging

crazily between right and left. In 1820, a popular rebellion forced a liberal constitution on the King—hence, by extension, on Mexico. The Mexican rich, abetted by their churchmen, thereupon resolved to sever connections with the mother country and quarantine the colony against liberal infection. This they did by simply proclaiming their independence. The church, which had hitherto opposed the very idea of such a thing, was now all for it.

The Spanish Viceroy had been raising an army to go after the last of the Morelos holdouts—old Vicente Guerrero and his band, holed up in the south but still organized, armed, and dangerous. To lead the expedition, the Viceroy chose Agustín Iturbide, a personable though unprincipled young Creole officer. Iturbide, although he had been in trouble for racketeering with army supplies, had a strong "in" with the church. Largely for this reason, he was picked (unbeknown to the Viceroy) to be the chosen tool of the Creole establishment in engineering its secretly decided-upon separation from Spain.

Iturbide marched against Guerrero but was unable to beat him. Indeed, he received a setback. He then resorted to diplomacy. The politically naive Guerrero was persuaded to join with Iturbide in liberating Mexico from the Spanish yoke. In early 1821, the unlikely pair promulgated the "Plan of Iguala"—named for the southern town in which it was published.

According to the terms of the plan, independence was proclaimed on the basis of three principles, or "guarantees": Mexican citizenship and equal rights for all, European and American-born; preservation of the Catholic faith, with toleration of no other creed; establishment of a constitutional monarchy, the throne to be offered to Ferdinand of Spain or, if he did not want it, to some other European prince. (Ferdinand, badgered by liberals at home, had been showing signs of wishing to leave Spain for Mexico.)

War-weary troops and civilians flocked like sheep to the

tricolor banner of the "three guarantees." The combined forces of Iturbide, Guerrero, and some of his insurgent leaders entered the capital in triumph. The Viceroy was relieved of his responsibility by the arrival of his successor; the new Viceroy arrived just in time to witness and accept the accomplished fact of independence. Having ratified this by treaty—which provided, among other things, for the repatriation of Spaniards and Spanish capital—he took the boat back to Spain.

One month after Iturbide entered the capital at the head of his troops, Benito Juárez entered the Catholic Seminary in Oaxaca at age fifteen.

1822–23

In the first efforts to reconstitute the colony as an independent country, conservative elements easily had the upper hand. A provisional governing board proclaimed the Mexican Empire in accordance with the provisions of Iguala— but not a single representative of the old insurgents was named to that board.

Iturbide, never one to be bashful, then substituted himself for European royalty. The simple device of having soldiers of his own regiment start a "spontaneous" street demonstration caught on like wildfire. In less than twenty-four hours, a docile congress had paid heed to the crowd and had ratified assumption of the crown by Agustín I.

The upstart Emperor soon dissolved that congress and made himself virtual dictator. Before long, he had lost all his bases of support. Spiraling inflation aggravated an increasingly intolerable situation. In 1823, Iturbide was overthrown by a military coup and banished. On his ill-advised return to Mexico a year later, he was captured and executed.

1824

By this time, the two main streams of Mexican politics were setting the course they were to follow for many a bitter decade. On the one side were the conservatives. They favored the centralization of power in a national government responsive to the desires of the establishment—the alliance of property, church, and army. The conservatives looked to absolutist Europe for inspiration and support.

On the other side were the liberals. They advocated a loose federation of states. They were committed to social justice and broader guarantees of the rights of the individual. They favored education of the masses and, of course, disestablishment of the church. They took as their guiding star the United States, whose "federal structure and . . . principles of liberty and progress" were, in Juárez' later words, "making prosperous and happy the neighboring republic . . . of the north."

Liberalism has always been a fractured philosophy at best. The Mexican liberals were at an especial disadvantage in the early days because they had had virtually no on-the-job experience. They had no idea how to go about transforming ideals and slogans into a working system of government. Discouragement caused frequent defections from their ranks. For the next three decades, the conservatives were destined to hold power with only a few noteworthy breaks.

Still, the fall of Iturbide's short-lived monarchy had a sort of backlash effect. The liberals did come to power in the beginning. In 1824, old insurgents were elected to both the presidency and the vice presidency of the new Mexican republic.

A constitution based on the U.S. model was drawn up and duly proclaimed. The conservative opposition was far from weak, however, and the new charter ended up as a compromise between progress and reaction. The administrative structure followed that of the United States, to be sure, and popular sovereignty was recognized—but the constitution of 1824 also reasserted the principle of ecclesiastical supremacy proclaimed in Iturbide's Plan of Iguala.

The insurgent movement had been inspired and led by two priests. Many of the lower, working clergy had rallied to it. Yet the church as an institution was still strong enough in 1824 to defy any challenge to its power for the foreseeable future. It had managed to maintain its imperial status by a timely moving-in on the independence movement.

A new nation had been born, but what was it? Independence had been won, but for whom and from what? The Spanish oligarchy was out, but, as far as the masses were concerned, the Creole establishment was not any different. The church still owned over half the wealth. Secular wealth remained in the hands of the few. Churchmen and the military still had feudal rights and privileges and were still judged in special courts by their peers.

Yet the insurgent priests had started something, and that something would not die. The successors of Hidalgo and Morelos soon realized that political independence was not the end but rather the beginning of the conflict. A new phase of the insurgent movement began—the fight for social liberation and the equality of all men under the law. It was to be a bitter struggle. To win it, to redeem the swindle of false independence, was clearly beyond the powers of any fledgling liberal government of the day, no matter how dedicated its leadership. That task was to fall to the next generation—the generation of Benito Juárez.

3

A Boy Leaves Home

ONE DECEMBER morning in 1818, a twelve-year-old Indian boy was watching over his uncle's small flock of sheep in the mountains of southern Mexico. Some men driving mules came toiling up the country road. They must have come from Oaxaca, thought the boy. When he found they had, he began to question them avidly about the big city below. His sister Josefa was there, in domestic service. Young Benito's cherished wish was to join her and start working for the education he was determined to get.

When the muleteers had gone their way, Benito got a rude shock. One of his sheep was missing. The small boy pondered his predicament somberly. How to face his uncle minus an animal? Just then, an older boy came down the road and confirmed Benito's fears. He also had met the mule-drivers, and they had a sheep with them.

That did it. Fear of what his uncle might do to him in the morning, plus his already firm determination not to pass his days as a backward village peasant, pushed the boy over a line; he was resolved to leave home. After a restless night, he pulled on his homemade grass cloak, faced the dawn, and, before dark, walked the forty miles to Oaxaca. Childhood was over. Benito Juárez had a hard, bare foot on the bottom rung of the ladder.

Benito Juárez

Some forty years later, when he was near the top of that ladder, Juárez produced his succinct but extensive *Notes for My Children*. It begins with a date that he doubtless got from the parish register of Santo Tomás Ixtlán, whither he was carried by his parents to be baptized:

> On March 21, 1806, I was born in the village of San Pablo Guelatao. . . . I had the misfortune of not knowing my parents, Marcelino Juárez and Brígida García, Indians of the primitive race of the country, because I had hardly reached three years of age when they died, leaving [me] with my sisters María Josefa and Rosa in the care of our paternal grandparents . . . also Indians of the Zapotec nation.

A few years later, the grandparents also died, and Benito was left in the care of his bachelor uncle, Bernardino. As soon as he was old enough, the child went to work in the fields. His uncle, fortunately, saw to it that Benito learned his letters. Only Zapotec was spoken in the village, however, and the boy soon perceived that the key to success was a knowledge of Spanish. For that, he would have to go to "the city."

For those like Benito who could not pay for schooling, the custom of the day was to enter domestic service—this in exchange for being taught to speak, read, and write the language of the masters. The boy often begged his uncle to take him to Oaxaca. Bernardino, apparently loath to part with his unpaid farm hand, kept putting him off. By the time he was twelve, Benito was ripe and ready for a break. When it came, even in such a negative guise as the sheep incident, he seized it forthwith. The hike to Oaxaca must have been a lonely and hungry one, but the small boy who made it was obeying the call of a far greater hunger—the longing for learning and a driving urge to amount to something.

When he got to Oaxaca, tired and empty, Benito had difficulty locating his sister. Not only did he know no Spanish,

but the Indians of Oaxaca were more likely to speak the related
Mixtec tongue than his native Zapotec. When he did at last find
Josefa, the reunion was a joyful one. His sister, though young,
had attained the exalted rank of cook in the household of don
Antonio Maza (originally, Mazza; he had emigrated from
Italy). The Mazas took to Benito at once and made him feel at
home. They were a warm, happy family, not rich but
prospering, and, evidently, far more easy and democratic than
their haughty Spanish counterparts. Not only did they befriend
the young Juárez as he grew to manhood, they eventually
became his parents-in-law.

After several weeks had passed, Señor Maza found Benito a
place in the home of don Antonio Salanueva, an elderly lay
brother. Juárez, in *Notes for My Children* (hereafter referred to
as *Notes* . . .), describes Salanueva as "a pious and very
honorable man who worked as a bookbinder. He wore the habit
of the Third Order of St. Francis and, although dedicated to
devotions and religious practices, was very broad-minded and
was a friend of the education of youth."

Don Antonio was indeed a man of honor and integrity. He
and Benito soon came to love one another. The old man saw to
it that his charge got what education was available, demanding
in return only such help around the house as Benito's studies
permitted. He also had him confirmed in church, thus
becoming his godfather.

What education was available in the Oaxaca of those days
was rather poor pickings, at least for a charity pupil in the
parish school. The Indian boys were not put in with the Creole
children. They were segregated in a back room without
teaching materials, where an "assistant" dealt out sketchy,
take-it-or-leave-it instruction in basic reading and writing—no
grammar—and devoted many hours to recital of the catechism.

Benito stuck stoically with it for about a year. Meanwhile, he
said nothing to his godfather lest the old man be hurt. (Don
Antonio had no idea of how the school was run.) Then the boy

took his courage in his hands and applied for transfer to a better unit of the system. This involved taking a writing test, in which Benito, naturally, made some errors. The man who marked the paper did not point these out or offer any helpful criticism. He simply lost his temper and had the boy punished.

"This injustice offended me deeply," wrote Juárez later on. We may well believe it. If there was one thing Benito Juárez could not stand, it was injustice in any form—to others as well as to himself. In any case, the boy decided then and there to leave school and try teaching himself. Don Antonio accepted this, and Benito spend several years working at home, surrounded by his godfather's many books. In his studies, he was aided by the light of a resin stump, a gift from the woman next door. It served as an after-dark auxiliary to his sharp young Indian eyes.

Despite his single-minded pursuit of learning, the young Benito was, by all accounts, a healthy, high-spirited boy. Reminiscences of his sometime playmates, collected at a much later date, give evidence that, despite his dedication, the boy did have his lighter moments. Many are the pranks recounted, with Benito cast in the role of ringleader—doubtless with some hindsight of history embellishing the retelling. He did not get much chance to blow off steam, but when he did, he made a good job of it.

Now well into his teens, Benito persevered and grew ready for the next step up the ladder. As he did so, he became increasingly aware of the many young men of his age going to and coming from the nearby Holy Cross Seminary. At the same time, he was struck by the "respect and consideration" shown by all classes of society, not only for priests but even for students preparing to become priests. Before long, he asked his godfather to get him into the seminary.

The old man was delighted. A staunch liberal and humanitarian, he was a convinced believer in Indian betterment. He also believed firmly in the need for more Indian-speaking priests. On October 18, 1821, with Salanueva's backing, Benito Juárez became one of the very few Indian students at the Oaxaca Seminary. As already noted, this was only a month after Agustín Iturbide entered Mexico City.

The fifteen-year-old Benito had no intention of becoming a priest. He was not against religion—far from it. Notwithstanding accusations of godlessness leveled by his enemies (even to this day), there is ample evidence that Benito Juárez was a devout Catholic as a youth, took virtue and goodness very seriously all his life, and believed in God till his death. He was very much on the side of the progressive clergy, from great Hidalgo and Morelos to modest Antonio Salanueva. Yet he felt "repugnance" for the church as he saw it operating in priest-ridden Oaxaca, where, as a respected Mexican historian later put it, there was always "exploitation of that poor person on his knees." Moreover, according to a noted French cleric who wrote some years later of his days in Mexico, celibacy of the clergy was largely a myth and vows of poverty a mockery.

Still, the young man wanted above all else to get ahead, with the realistic approach (later to be called ruthless ambition by some) that came naturally to him. And, at the seminary, get ahead he did. Finally, in his twenty-first year, the time was drawing nigh when he must either cross the clerical Rubicon or draw back from it. Then came the break he had unconsciously been waiting for. A secular institution of learning opened in Oaxaca.

We have already noted that the liberals came to power after the fall of Iturbide. One of their most cherished goals was to break the church's monopoly on education, principally by founding lay schools to emancipate the coming generation. Even in traditional Oaxaca, liberals gained a majority in the legislature. In 1827, they created the Institute of Arts and Science.

At the outset, there were many transfers from the seminary to the institute. The new school offered an approach to learning unfettered by the bonds of dogma or theological accommodation. Out of deference to his godfather's feelings, however, young Juárez finished his theology course at the seminary before transferring to the institute in 1828. Even so, it must have been a painful moment for don Antonio when he realized that his beloved godson had, in effect, been stringing along with the priesthood plan just to get an education.

The young man had the makings of a good politician, however, and was already adept at handling people. His genuine affection for his godfather, aided by discernment and tact, enabled him to get his way without hurting the old man overmuch.

The new institute was pretty much a do-it-yourself operation. The professors were not far ahead of their pupils, and, before long, some of the latter were doubling as substitute instructors. And, although the director and some of the professors were in holy orders, they were of the same priestly breed that had produced Hidalgo and Morelos. Their approach to learning was untrammeled by mumbo jumbo. Their approach to politics was partisan and involved.

Under the circumstances, it is not surprising that the establishment soon cracked down on what it could not help but view as a hotbed of heresy and subversion. Juárez, in his *Notes . . .* , tells us that the clergy,

> using the very powerful influence that it exercised at that time on the civil authority, on families, and on all of society, declared a systematic and cruel war on the new institution. They called the Institute a house of prostitution, and the professors and students heretics and libertines.

With such heat put on them, many students deserted. This made those who remained all the more tightly knit in their resolve to stick it out. Among their number were quite a few who were later to play a role in the world of Juarist politics.

It was during this period that the brilliant young firebrand professor Miguel Méndez—himself a Zapotec, who, like Juárez, had pulled himself up by his bootstraps—began holding informal get-togethers in his rooms to argue and thrash out plans for Mexico's future. At one of these sessions, according to local tradition, the intense and fever-bright Méndez—he was prey to t.b. and not long for the world—dramatically pointed his finger at the silent Juárez and cried: "And this one whom you see here, so serious and reserved, this one will be a great politician. He will rise higher than any of us, and he will be one of our great men and the glory of our country."

It was also during Juárez' student days, in 1829, that another crossed his path who foresaw no such glories. This was the opportunist Antonio López de Santa Anna.

In 1828, at the end of the first four-year liberal administration, chaos reigned in the land. After many marchings and countermarchings, the right man, Vicente Guerrero, was made president by the wrong method—by bullets, not ballots. A Creole officer who had fought for the Viceroy against the insurgents, "General" Santa Anna had made a name for himself during the confusion by playing both ends against the middle. He had changed sides from the Viceroy to Iturbide; then, when the latter started slipping, he became a "republican." In 1828, he jumped on the Guerrero bandwagon just in time.

A darling of the liberals at the moment, Santa Anna was given a testimonial dinner by their leaders in Oaxaca. A young student waiter named Benito Juárez was among those who served at table.

Santa Anna, who had the politician's gift for names and faces, somehow fixed on the young Indian and remembered him in later life, when he wrote: "He could not forgive me because he had waited on me at table in Oaxaca, in December, 1829, with his bare feet on the floor and in his linen smock and trousers. . . . It is amazing that an Indian of such low degree should have become the figure in Mexico that we all know."

Juárez, although he was certainly aware of the identity of the guest of honor, could surely not have cared less about their relative positions at the time. Later, the two almost destroyed one another.

At the institute, Juárez majored in law and minored in science. By 1830, he was substituting for the physics professor while continuing his law studies. In these, he was sufficiently qualified a year later to enter a law office—though he did not pass the bar examinations until 1834.

In those days, as throughout modern times, the law was an overcrowded profession. It was looked upon more often as a passport to politics than as a means of earning a livelihood. In 1831, Benito Juárez first ran for public office—successfully—and was elected municipal alderman. At age twenty-five, the young Zapotec had his foot, still hard but no longer bare, on one more rung of the ladder.

4

The Judge Takes a Wife

THE YOUNG republic went from upheaval to upheaval. For the next two decades, power was seized by a succession of windbag politicos, gangsters in gold braid, and—from time to time—honest, able men. The liberals represented the wave of the future—history has shown us that—but, even when briefly in power, they were still too few and too inexperienced to be effective. The honest conservatives—and these did not lack—were inhibited by their ties with the church, the army, and the propertied. The economy was underdeveloped, and kept so. Both sides marched and countermarched, plotted and counterplotted. The apathetic masses—at least those who were able to remain noncombatant—looked on with indifference.

Physically, the Mexican scene had changed little from that of colonial times. Great stone palaces sparsely furnished, ramshackle huts with earthen floors and, often, a small flower bed. Bullfights and banquets, hangings and hunger. So it had been in 1810. So it was to be for many decades to come.

Equally enduring was to be the institution of the *pronunciamiento,* whereby chieftains big and small "pronounced" against a regime national or local, published a platform or "plan," and went into armed insurrection.

How did these pronouncers live? Where did they get their

arms, clothing, food? It must be borne in mind that Mexico in those days was still largely a feudal land. Every estate was like a self-sufficient fortress, making its own weapons and ammunition—crude but effective—growing and storing its own food. It wove its own cloth, much of it from the common cactus—which also provided the soldier with hats and knapsacks, leaves to cook food in, and beer and distilled firewater to keep him going. The peasant on campaign could march and fight on the beans and tortillas he carried in his knapsack. Any bits of meat he could steal or shoot en route were windfall.

Few of those who pronounced had peasant armies of their own. Like Morelos, they got help from those who did. Allegiance was personal rather than political. As in medieval Europe, when the lord of the manor joined a cause and called his men out to fight, they went. More than one of Mexico's hauntingly beautiful folk songs, still sung today, echoes the theme of sad departure: the singer must leave his beloved, must go forth to obey the call of his lord and master.

In this brief volume, I shall leave out the marchings and pronouncements, except insofar as they bear directly on the Juárez story. They should be borne in mind, nonetheless, as a continuing backdrop to events that are given the spotlight.

In 1830, the old insurgent Vicente Guerrero was deposed by a conservative coup, caught and publicly humiliated, then shot. Anastasio Bustamante, who took over as president, ruled with an increasingly heavy hand. Before long he had more enemies than friends. The soldier of fortune, Santa Anna, sniffing the winds of discontent, touched off a series of provincial insurrections that ended in the overthrow of the conservative regime. In 1833, he was made president.

Here began what has been called the reign of Santa Anna. This colorful in-and-outer (he assumed power, then dropped it again, five times in twenty years) has provided rich descriptive inspiration to historians. A few examples: mountebank, upstart, perpetual turncoat, unprincipled opportunist, attractive, daring, great organizing ability, unmitigated cheek, reckless ambition, overweening conceit—and fat little man. To the Texans of 1836, he was "that Santy Anny." His incompetent overconfidence was to blame for many a disaster. His life style was corrupt and incontinent. In political theory, he was an illiterate. Yet he had the finger-tip sensitivity of a master political operator.

Once he had the presidency, Santa Anna thought it well to leave the hard work to others. He withdrew to his country estate, to rest on his laurels and indulge his passion for cockfights and the bullring. This left the country in the interim charge of his Vice President, the physician Valentín Gómez Farías, co-author of the constitution and a flat-out liberal.

Under Gómez Farías and his political-philosophic mentor, José Luis Mora, Mexico briefly witnessed a false dawn of liberal reform. Benito Juárez, as one of the party's young comers, was caught in the liberal updraft and took a few more steps up the political ladder. In 1833, he was elected to the Oaxaca state legislature. In 1834, a few days after passing his bar examination, he was made an acting magistrate and held the office "for a short time."

Also during this period, in 1833, the young man saw brief but active volunteer service in the militia, defending Oaxaca against an unsuccessful conservative siege. (He reached the rank of captain.) Aside from earlier volunteer service during his days as a student, this was Juárez' only experience in uniform.

Santa Anna dallied away his days as a country gentleman. The liberal leaders in the capital, backed by a like-minded congress, piled reform on radical reform. Education was secularized, the university disestablished. Certain of the lesser ecclesiastical prerogatives were taken over by the state.

Conservative consternation grew. The church felt itself threatened. The build-up to crisis was given a good boost by a runaway cholera epidemic, in which the clergy did not fail to point out the hand of a jealous and wrathful God.

At last, Santa Anna grew bored with life in the country. With a fine sense of timing, he allowed himself to be talked into returning to the capital. There, he set himself up as dictator, neatly turned his coat within what was nominally his own party, and jammed the helm 180 degrees to the right. Reform legislation was repealed, the liberal leaders exiled, and the rank and file thrown out of office. With them went the young Zapotec lawyer of Oaxaca.

Such was the changing backdrop to the episode at Loxicha°, an early milestone on the political path of Benito Juárez.

Juárez, already known as one who defended the poor, was appealed to for help by the villagers of a hamlet near Loxicha, some 60 miles south of Oaxaca. Their parish priest, they said, was extorting payments and demanding services far beyond established rates. The young barrister studied reports and documents, decided the villagers had a case, and took it.

This meant appearing before an ecclesiastical court in Loxicha, which he did. (It should be noted that this was in early 1834, with the liberals still in power.) Juárez was a member of both legislature and judiciary—a man of status. Doubtless because of this, the petition was accepted by the church court. The priest was ordered to answer charges and was forbidden to return to his parish until the matter had been cleared up.

Before the trial took place, however, the liberal administration was thrown out. Juárez was without status. The case collapsed. The priest returned to his parish and had all who had complained against him arrested and held incommunicado. Juárez, now only a substitute professor of canonical law at the Institute of Arts and Science, was indignant. He requested a few days' leave and hurried to the village.

On arrival, he was allowed to see his clients. On the next day, a curtain had been rung down. He was told to drop the case and threatened with jail on a vagrancy charge if he did not. Seeing

°"Loxicha" today; "Loricha" in the time of Juárez, who so spells it in his *Notes* . . .

the deck stacked against him in Loxicha, he returned to Oaxaca and set out to press charges through civil channels.

The priest had got there ahead of him, however, and secured a writ for Juárez' arrest on grounds of inciting the villagers against the authorities. Juárez was thrown in jail. Although he appealed to the Superior Court, it was nine days before he could get out on bail. To add insult to injury, no further account was taken of the charges he had pressed. And for the hapless villagers—whose only crime had been to complain of illegal treatment—the doors of justice remained closed.

Juárez, in his *Notes . . .* , tells us that this experience "of the arbitrary acts of the privileged classes in close association with the civil authority . . . confirmed me in my resolution to work unceasingly to destroy the baneful power of the privileged classes." When he took the case, Benito Juárez was a promising young politician, busy making his mark. By the time it had bogged down in a dead end of injustice, he was a reformer for life.

It was to be some time before the conversion would begin to show. For one thing, the young man had to live. With the liberals out of power, he was only a teaching substitute and a struggling barrister in an overcrowded profession—and one who specialized in poor clients to boot.

It was in this period before marriage that the young lawyer fathered the only two illegitimate children of which there is record (and this only in Juárez' own correspondence). The daughter, Susana, became an invalid and was addicted to drugs. In Juárez' later years, she was in the care of an old friend and sometime governor of Oaxaca. The son, Tereso, fought against the Imperialists and was taken prisoner in 1863. We have no further record of his fate.

Juárez, in his letters, made no secret of his concern for the welfare of both. Their existence, if noted by others, would certainly have raised no eyebrows.

Despite the odds against him in Oaxaca of the mid-1830's,

Juárez managed to progress in his private practice and his teaching. He became respectable. In time, he was offered professional and political appointments by the conservative regime—and accepted them.

In 1841, he was appointed to the bench. In 1843, he made the marriage that was to provide a never failing source of strength and peace. The following year, he accepted a position as secretary to the conservative Governor of Oaxaca—an erstwhile follower of Morelos, but now a satellite of Santa Anna. When it came to signing an order that went against his principles, Juárez resigned. Yet he did not suffer for his stand. He was made a state prosecutor and, soon thereafter, was seated on the state Supreme Court. In 1845, he was again elected to the state legislature.

Margarita Juárez

(Photograph from the collection of María Cristina Sánchez Juárez, granddaughter of don Benito)

For all his subsequent words about the baneful association of civil authority and privileged classes, Benito Juárez, in 1845, was considered a safe man. It is not surprising that his critics, both contemporary and latter-day, point to this period as evidence that the god of reform had his feet of clay. Few, however, have questioned his probity in office. And, as we shall see before long, his dormant reformist zeal—born at Loxicha, then suppressed for a score of timeserving years—was destined to be reborn with a bang. Before going into that, let us take a side trip into the land of true romance.

"On July 31, 1843," Juárez wrote for his children: "I married doña Margarita Maza, daughter of don Antonio Maza and of doña Petra Parada." Behind this brief entry lies a heartwarming story of love and honor.

In the years since the Maza family had taken in their cook's small brother, protectors and protected had become fast friends. Young Benito often found a haven of peace in the warmth of the Maza family life. When he was twenty years old, and still at the seminary, the Mazas were blessed with a new addition to the clan—a girl child whom they named Margarita. Young Juárez, as a close friend of the family and a frequent dropper-in, doubtless baby-sat and played with her often.

When she reached sixteen, he suddenly realized that Margarita was no longer a child but a comely young lady. As tradition has it, this was borne in on him one evening when he noticed a would-be suitor walking back and forth beneath her parlor window. The young man was following the Latin custom, observed in Mexico, of "playing the bear"—openly declaring his intentions. Tradition further has it that on another evening, not many weeks later, a certain more mature character, with stovepipe hat and straight black cane, was out in front of the Mazas' doing the same.

Margarita saw nothing absurd in the ursine antics of the middle-aged judge. She loved him too. Soon, she prevailed upon her father to ask him in. This was a sign that his suit was acceptable, to father as well as to daughter.

When they were married, Juárez was thirty-seven; Margarita, seventeen. The union of self-made judge and well-born bride was accepted by Oaxaca society as matter-of-factly as it was by Margarita herself. The words she used to describe him have been preserved, and show forth her whole heart: "He is very homely but very good."

Benito Juárez was a lucky man. His lady took in stride a life often fraught with hardship, heartache, and danger. She was a woman of spirit, and doubtless they had their differences. Yet she never failed him, nor he her. Their love was deep and true, and they remained devoted to each other until death.

5

The Governor at Work

BEFORE RETURNING to the alarums and excursions of mid-century Mexico, let us extend our side trip to include a brief look at Benito Juárez the man. Of contemporary descriptions, one of the most expressive is that of Juárez as president by the American-born Princess Salm-Salm, who, as we shall see later, had several harrowing interviews with him in an effort to save the life of Maximilian of Habsburg:

> Juarez is a man a little under the middle size, with a very dark complexioned Indian face, which is not disfigured, but, on the contrary, made more interesting by a very large scar across it. He has very black piercing eyes, and gives one the impression of being a man who reflects much, and deliberates long and carefully before acting. He wore high old English collars and a black neck-tie, and was dressed in black broadcloth.

"A little under the middle size" was not much more than five feet, according to a well-informed source. His body was strong and stocky, and an American officer (on border duty in 1865) commented on his "fine head, and remarkably small hands and feet." Other sources have confirmed the Princess's remark on the penetrating quality of his eyes. The "very large scar" was, in fact, short and deep, a childhood cut on the upper lip that shows on Juárez' death mask. The black coat and black bow tie, and, with them, the straight black cane that was his constant companion, were part of the Juárez picture—as were the fine white shirts that often were made by his wife. Through all the ins and outs of a hectic life, he dressed neatly and bathed daily whenever he could. He carried a side arm only when he thought he would need it.

Juárez' manner with others was low-key, often gently ironic but always kind and considerate. Women referred to his way with them as sweet. His modest reserve sometimes led opponents to underestimate him. Those who did so learned better. He ate sparingly, drank only a little wine. His vice was cigars, which he smoked whenever he could get them. Possibly tobacco helped him to "deliberate long and carefully before acting"—as he was certainly known to do.

While Benito Juárez was busy making his mark in Oaxaca politics, the national scene continued in futile ferment. Internal disorganization and partisan strife made stability and progress impossible. Meanwhile, storm clouds were gathering to the north.

The United States had had designs on what is now Texas since before Mexican independence, and it was moving in. By the mid-1830's, some 50,000 of the area's 68,000 people were Americans. Border bickering began.

In 1833, Santa Anna sent an army north. It was defeated by Texan partisans. In 1836, the President himself led another army up to San Antonio, where he butchered the defenders of the Alamo. A few months later, at San Jacinto, Sam Houston caught him napping (literally this was so; Santa Anna was having a siesta and was captured in his carpet slippers). The Mexican, ever fertile in expedient, soon made a deal: his freedom in exchange for recognizing Texan independence. Back in Mexico, he was disavowed—naturally—and removed from office.

Again, Santa Anna retired to country life, near the port of Veracruz. In 1838, though out of power, he got himself mixed up in rather a comic-opera episode with French raiders and lost a leg below the knee. Four years later, when he was back in power, the leg was dug up. In a ceremony that by all accounts was unrivaled for bathos, it was solemnly reburied with full military honors.

Mexico continued on its collision course with itself. Texas existed nine years as a republic, denied admission to the Union because the North resisted taking in another slave state. Santa Anna, back in power, threatened to reconquer the territory. The Texans appealed for help to Great Britain. This jolted the U.S. Government into annexing the state into the Union in 1845.

There was trigger-happiness on both sides of the border. Soon the chips were down. In April, 1846, General Zachary Taylor was ordered to march south to the Rio Grande (*Rio Bravo del Norte* to the Mexicans). Ulysses S. Grant, then a lieutenant, wrote, later, in his memoirs: "We were sent to provoke a fight, but it was essential that Mexico should commence it." Mexico did. American blood was spilt. The United States declared war.

There is no need to go into the details of the campaign. Suffice it to say that, for two years, Mexicans and Americans fought with courage and resourcefulness, that Mexico's disorganization and unpreparedness made defeat inevitable, and that, for just $15 million, the United States ended up with all of Mexico north of the Rio Grande—nearly half its territory. It was an ugly little war. Even today, few Mexicans are without some bitterness about it. Many thoughtful Americans, from that day down to this, have felt some guilt about the U.S. role—and recognize, perforce, that Mexico has grounds for its recurrent suspicion of and hostility toward the Colossus of the North.

Let us return to Benito Juárez and his role in this hour of crisis. In 1846, shortly before war broke out, the conservative grip on national power was broken. In Oaxaca, a liberal coalition set up a caretaker triumvirate to govern provisionally. Juárez was one of the three. That he was chosen was a tribute to his earlier liberal record, but his collaboration with the conservatives could not be entirely overlooked. When the time came to choose one of the trio as governor, the choice fell not on Juárez but on one who had stuck with the liberals throughout.

On the national scene, it was the liberal Gómez Farías, back from exile, who took over as acting president. Not for long. Santa Anna, out of power for two years, soon popped up like a jack-in-the-box and took over. With a war on their hands, the liberals felt the need for a leader of heroic proportions. And for all his phoniness, Santa Anna did operate on a grandiose and charismatic scale.

A special congress, originally convoked to revise the constitution, became transformed into a war congress of national emergency. Juárez, as one of the nine deputies elected from his state, was swept from the provincial circuit into the big time. On what was apparently his first trip to Mexico City, the new congressman from Oaxaca arrived in the capital early in December, 1846. Another step up the ladder.

By contemporary accounts, Juárez did not find himself much at home in the parliamentary milieu. His colleagues remembered him as a sphinx. At congressional sessions (though not in the corridors), he limited his speech to a laconic yea or nay to the business at hand. The oratory he left to others. And orate the others did, at great length and with little advantage to the national interest.

The national interest, meanwhile, was going to hell in a handbasket. While congress wrangled, the Yankee invaders overran the north and pushed toward the capital. Santa Anna threw together a fresh army, pledged his personal property with a great flourish, and cast about for larger and better-heeled sources of funds.

His eye lit on the church. He decided it must disgorge some of its gains. The dirty work of making it do so, however, he prudently left to the congress liberals under Vice President Gómez Farías.

The brunt of the funding job fell to the deputies from Oaxaca. At a time when Representative Abraham Lincoln of Illinois was condemning the Mexican war in principle while voting money to carry it on, Deputy Benito Juárez of Oaxaca was doing his best to raise money for the fighting men of Mexico. The Oaxaca delegation introduced and pushed through a resolution empowering the government to mortgage church property, to the value of $15 million, for prosecution of the war.°

The church soon took its revenge. Putting primacy above patriotism, the clergy put pressure on a crack regiment to mutiny and overthrow the government—this on the very eve of its departure to bolster the defense of hard-pressed Veracruz.

This Revolt of the *Polkos*—as the pietistic fops who officered the turncoat regiment were called—evoked immediate and indignant citizen reaction. The capital was in a state of virtual civil war. The government was paralyzed. The rebels got to Santa Anna, who came charging back from the front.

Although he had just been handed another defeat in the field, Santa Anna was hailed as a conquering hero by clergy and mutineers. Juárez, in his *Notes . . .*, comments dryly that the rebels "went to the town of Guadalupe to receive their protector, with their chests covered with badges of membership in religious orders and relics of saints." Santa Anna repealed the assessment that had originally been his own idea, fired his front man Gómez Farías, and took over in person. Once again, out went the liberals.

This exercise in subversion cost the church far more in the long run than if it had paid up in the first place. Not only did the clergy end by paying Santa Anna considerably more than

---

°Mexican peso amounts will be stated in U.S. dollars throughout. In Juárez' time, the peso was worth almost a dollar.

had been requested by congress; they also suffered a serious setback to their moral authority and in public respect. More and more ordinary Mexicans began to see their church for what it then was—a self-serving operation acknowledging neither civil nor civic obligations.

In Oaxaca, the Revolt of the *Polkos* produced its local counterpart. The clerical-conservative element captured the state government. In Mexico City, the Oaxaca deputies did not take this lying down—even though congress was as good as dissolved. By dint of bargaining, buttonholing, and skillful parliamentary infighting, the delegation ("on my motion and that of my associates," as Juárez put it) pushed through a congressional resolution condemning the Oaxaca mutiny and refusing to recognize the rebel authorities.

There was no way of enforcing this resolution from Mexico City, nor was any attempt made to do so. Still, it had the force of law. That was enough for Benito Juárez. The law, as he said in an oft-repeated quote, had always been his sword and his shield.

After the liberal defeat in congress, Juárez decided, in August of 1847, to go home and play it by ear—meanwhile resuming his law practice. Although the conservatives held the power, he found Oaxaca's liberal strength very much alive and kicking. So successful was he in buckling on the sword and shield of the law and marshaling liberal resources that two months later he was able to write that "we succeeded very well in a movement against the intruding authorities. The President of the Court of Justice, Lic. don Marcos Pérez, took charge of the government; the legislature met and named me Governor *pro tempore* of the state."

Thus, Benito Juárez, one year past forty, placed his foot on the key rung of the ladder that was his career. Not the highest rung, but the most significant. He had at last got himself matched up with the job to which he was best suited—that of running a government. He was destined, through many ups and downs, to spend the best part of his remaining days at that job.

On October 29, 1847, "I assumed the power [as Governor] which I exercised provisionally until August 12, 1848, when the powers of the state were reconstituted," Juárez wrote for his children. "I was then reelected for the second constitutional period, which ended in August, 1852."

Juárez was a good governor. To the administration of postwar Oaxaca he gave an outstanding example of what could be achieved by honesty, thrift, and sound management. In due course, the country began to take notice.

He looked upon his state as his family. There was a big job to be done, and the whole family must roll up sleeves and pitch in. Juárez practiced what he preached. His lead was followed, and he got results.

Inner convictions or no inner convictions, Juárez was not yet ready to make war on the church—nor had the church yet declared war on him. At his inauguration in 1847, the new Governor took the customary oath of office. It bound him to defend and uphold the constitution and the laws, and—furthermore—to defend and preserve the Catholic religion. While he was governor, Juárez lived up to his oath—not only because he had sworn it but also because he needed the cooperation of that other government that was the church. Within foreseeable limits, he got it.

Another human relations problem, of an entirely different order, was that of his own people, the Indians. A delegation from his home town trooped down the mountainside to his inauguration. They offered not only gifts—fruit, fowl, corn—but also their trust. "You know what we need, and you will give it to us," said their spokesman, one of Juárez' first cousins, "because you are good and will not forget that you are one of us."

The new Governor replied forthcomingly, embraced the delegates, and made them welcome. And he lived up to their trust in him—not by yielding to temptation and preferring them above others, but by working for their assimilation into the community and the raising of their living standard.

Above all, he gave top priority to education for the masses. At his second inauguration, in 1849, he echoed the Indian delegation's words when he said: "As a son of the people, I will not forget them; on the contrary, I will uphold their rights, I will see to it that they become educated, lift themselves up, and make a future for themselves."

When he took office, Juárez moved with his growing brood into a large colonial house in downtown Oaxaca. As restored today, it shows the massive stone proportions of Spanish colonial times. Its one great door opening into a patio recalls the Moorish occupation of Spain. Every morning, the Governor walked to work, arriving just as the cathedral bells struck nine. The people of Oaxaca did not know what to make of such punctuality, associated in their minds with common laborers rather than high officials. Yet it did not take long for his staff to get the message. They, too, began arriving on time and putting in a full day's work.

For as long as the war continued, the Governor's first priority was defense—against internal as well as external threat. As noted above, however, education was Juárez' key project and the one closest to his heart. "Education is the primary base of a people's prosperity," he said, "and at the same time the surest means for making abuses of power impossible."

Juárez, as governor, is credited with having built well over 200 schools, including eight normal schools, in Oaxaca state. Many Indian teachers were trained and employed. Pupil registration increased manyfold. In encouraging schooling for girls, Juárez was well ahead of his time.

The Governor also attached importance to road building, not only to ease the passage of goods and ideas but also to provide employment. Volunteer laborers were permitted to substitute road service for military service. In public works, he was able to enlist the cooperation of the church. Parish priests pitched in to enlist volunteers and help ride herd on projects. The high point of the program was the completion of a road to the Pacific. At the opening ceremony, the clergy fully participated. A church and a school were consecrated together. Outdoor Mass was sung on a peak looking down on the sea.

Juárez attempted nothing revolutionary, nothing spectacular. He introduced rotation and variation of crops into the state and did much to modernize the bureaucracy—especially, the antiquated customs service. His approach was always pragmatic. When he tried to revive the mining industry, he found himself stymied by a British concession, forgot it, and tried something else. The keystone of his arch of achievement, on which all other accomplishments depended, was fiscal integrity. In the five years of his stewardship, the state's debt was reduced from over $124,000 to under $9,000. This he managed principally by enforcing the tax law, collecting all taxes that were legal, and—most importantly—spending the money collected in legal ways. Also, unlike most state governors, he paid in his due share to the federal government.

With fiscal integrity came bureaucratic integrity. Civil servants were paid adequately and on time—hence, were less tempted to resort to the classic *mordida* ("bite"), which some Latin bureaucrats still put on the private sector today. The courts, especially, improved in both ethics and efficiency.

Needless to say, the Governor did not accomplish all these things sitting at a big desk in the Statehouse. He was a man of the people, and he got out among the people. When there was high-level troubleshooting to be done, he went out and did it himself. In 1850, for example, when a mutiny broke out in the battalion stationed in Oaxaca City, Juárez, himself, went down to where the shooting was. Armed with nothing but his straight black cane and his dignity, he coolly faced the rebels down.

A confrontation of a different sort, however, was to have more serious and lasting results. In late 1847, Mexico City was about to fall to the Americans. Santa Anna, with his highly developed sense of self-preservation, left the battle to his comrades-in-arms and took off south. Word came to Juárez that he was about to enter the upper limits of the state of Oaxaca.

According to the *Notes* . . . , news of Santa Anna's approach stimulated opposition elements within Oaxaca—already plotting some sort of coup—to send out agents urging the leader to come quickly. City council and legislature begged Juárez to forestall this. The Governor, therefore, sent word to the border that Santa Anna might transit the state, even stay a while, but must not come near the capital. The fugitive did, in fact, sojourn briefly upstate, then withdrew to the north without making trouble.

Many have assumed that Juárez forbade Santa Anna the capital on his own initiative and out of personal animosity. If we are to believe Juárez' own unimpassioned account, this was far from the case. As in 1829, when the student Juárez waited on him at table, the sensitivity was all on Santa Anna's side. He never forgave a slight, real or fancied, and, in this case, he chose to consider himself rebuffed. Six years later he was to take his revenge.

6

Exile

WHILE BENITO Juárez labored to rehabilitate postwar Oaxaca, Mexico as a whole was trying, without success, to pull itself together. There was general depression, both moral and economic. Bandits roamed the countryside undeterred. There were uprisings of back-country Indians in the north and south. Texans filibustered in and out without hindrance. With mines and farms so long neglected, commerce was at a virtual standstill. The $15-million indemnity from the United States was soon spent. The British, concerned over Mexico's longstanding and self-multiplying debt, renegotiated it on terms that made Mexico City an economic dependency of London.

From 1848 to 1853, Presidents Joaquín Herrera and Mariano Arista, both ex-generals, who were able and honest, worked near-miracles to stave off bankruptcy. In cutting expenses, however, Arista went too far in paring down the army. Various generals in the provinces pronounced against him, and he resigned in disgust.

The alliance of property, sacristy, and barracks, fishing in waters they themselves had helped to roil, moved in and ousted Arista's moderate successor, Juan Bautista Ceballos. The

51

presidency was assumed by a distinguished conservative intellectual, Lucas Alamán.

Alamán, though brilliant, was more ideologist than leader. Once again the party in power—this time the conservatives— felt the need for a strong man. Strong men were scarce in postwar Mexico. Once again, the nod went to the eternal Santa Anna. That hardy perennial left a pleasant exile and, at age fifty-eight, returned once more to the charge. He was soon back in his old form, splurging like a drunken sailor on pomp and circuses, banquets and bullfights. Alamán, as his chief minister, was able to restrain the glorious leader for a while, but in a very few months Alamán gave up and died.

One of Santa Anna's first steps was to rid the country of subversives. High on his list were two names. One was that of Melchor Ocampo, the iconoclast aristocrat who had made national headlines—favorable or unfavorable, depending on which paper you read—by his all-out liberal administration as governor of Michoacán. The other was that of one whom Santa Anna had never forgiven a fancied rebuff—the ex-governor of Oaxaca.

In 1852, his term as governor completed, Juárez had been made director of the Institute of Arts and Science and had also resumed his law practice. The institute job paid only $500 a year, but money was no particular problem at the time. Doña Margarita's dowry had included a country house in the Oaxaca suburb of Etla, and, more recently, her mother had died and left them some money.

By late 1852, the conservative-backed uprisings against Arista were already under way. A general who had served the liberal administration changed sides and was made governor of Oaxaca. Soon, Juárez was removed from the directorship of the institute.

Before that happened, a bizarre little incident took place that reflected the way things were in Oaxaca. The new Governor got a certain Máximo Ortiz to rent a house across

from Juárez' in order to keep tabs on his movements. This Ortiz
had been one of Juárez' *compadres* (in Mexico, a close
relationship, usually denoting the godparenthood of one to a
child of the other) but the two had fallen out politically. In
March, 1853, while don Benito and his wife were relaxing on
their balcony, Ortiz came down the street in disguise and took a
potshot at him.

He missed and ran into his own house. Juárez buckled on his
pistol and crossed the street. Ortiz' wife said he was not in. In a
loud voice, which Ortiz could not help but hear, Juárez called
out: "Tell my *compadre* that if he wants to kill me he should
come out, so that he can do it face to face!"

This was shortly before Santa Anna's takeover. Two months
later, when the dictator was back in power, he took vengeance
on Juárez. It was quick and dirty.

Juárez still had many clients among the poor. From time to
time, he went circuit-riding about the district, probably in
sober lawyer's garb, on horseback. His riding boots, preserved
today, suggest this sort of use. In May, 1853, he set out to collect
needed information. On May 27, when he was busy taking
testimony in Etla, soldiers appeared and arrested him. No
explanations were given, but he was issued orders to be
confined in Jalapa. This was the capital of Veracruz state, and a
Santa Anna stronghold. Without being permitted to say
farewells, even to wife and children, Juárez was taken to Jalapa
under cavalry guard. He was held under house arrest for
seventy-five days.

During that period, he was shunted about and chivvied by
conflicting orders to be moved and not to be moved. His
protests went unheeded. As he himself remarks in *Notes* . . . ,
he was like the lamb in the fable in which the wolf complained
that the lamb was muddying the wolf's water.

On the seventy-sixth day, José Santa Anna, son of the
dictator, came and took Juárez to the barracks jail. Thence, he
was sent under escort—all this incommunicado—on a ten-day

trip that ended at the fortress of San Juan de Ulúa in Veracruz harbor. The fortress had a dank and sinister dungeon, below sea level, and there he was kept for twelve days in solitary confinement. His health did not benefit.

Finally, on October 9, Juárez was called before the governor of the castle, informed that he was to be exiled to Europe, and handed a passport. He protested that he was ill and in no condition to travel. This got him nowhere. Without further ado, he was bundled onto an English steamer that was about to sail. No provision had been made for his passage, and he was penniless. When the passengers found out who he was, they took up a collection to pay his fare as far as Havana, the first port of call.

"I arrived at Havana," Juárez says in *Notes* . . . , "where by permission of the Captain General, Cañedo, I remained until the 18th of December [1853] when I embarked for New Orleans, arriving there on the 29th of the same month."

Doña Margarita, meanwhile, was being badgered by agents of the Governor. For a while, she hid out with the children. After some time, she was able to move to the house at Etla, where she set up a shop to help make ends meet. Somehow, she got word that her husband was in the Veracruz dungeon. She managed to borrow $400 from a friend and sent it off by safe hand of her brother, José María Maza. By the time Maza got to Veracruz, Juárez had been deported. Agents of Santa Anna confiscated his $400, but two foreign businessman friends (one Spanish, one Italian), somehow retrieved the money for him. Maza then set out by sea in an effort to catch up with his brother-in-law. He did so in Havana.

This summary deportation became the second and definitive milestone on the path of Juárez the reformer. The first, his experience at Loxicha in 1834, had sown a seed. The seed had been a late bloomer. Unnourished, it had lain deep and dormant, awaiting a stimulus.

Following his collaboration with the conservatives, Juárez

had achieved great things as liberal governor of Oaxaca, to be sure—but they were not revolutionary things. At age forty-seven he was a solid citizen, an honest and able administrator, a safe man who got the job done and got along with all sides to do so. Then—bango! Picked up and bounced out of the country, cut off from family, friends, security, Benito Juárez—through the caprice of a tinpot dictator—was at last put back on the rails of his life's mission.

Ironically for Santa Anna, Juárez never really understood the reason for his proscription. The tone of *Notes . . .* makes it clear that he attached so little importance to the border incident of 1847 that he failed to connect it directly to the events of 1853. He could see that Santa Anna was out to get him—naturally—but put it down to the dirty politics of enemies closer to home.

Thus Antonio López de Santa Anna, through pique suffered over an imagined insult, played out his personal little Greek tragedy and became the instrument of his own doom. Those he exiled, with Juárez high among them, gravitated to New Orleans to form the hard core of the reform movement. Once that got going, the days of Santa Anna were numbered.

The New Orleans exiles, a frequently changing group, included men who were soon to be among the new leaders of Mexico. Foremost was Melchor Ocampo, a personable and gifted gentleman, who had had all the advantages that Juárez had not—though he lacked the Indian's iron will and inexhaustible self-confidence. An aristocrat and landowner, he had made his mark as a scholar and a botanist before entering politics. As Juárez had done in Oaxaca, Ocampo, as governor of Michoacán, pulled his state together and mobilized it for the American war. He also had his "priest of Loxicha," but was strongly placed enough to bring the case into the open and make it a *cause célèbre.* His liberal friends ran him for president in 1851, against Arista.

In 1852, despite the implacable enmity of the church,

Ocampo was called back to the governorship. He then carried his progressive social reforms to such lengths that proscription by Santa Anna—or, indeed, by any conservative regime in power—was logical and inevitable. Ocampo and Juárez apparently overlapped as guests of honor in the dungeons of San Juan de Ulúa—although, both being in solitary, they did not meet.

Others among the exiles bear mentioning. Ponciano Arriaga, of whom Juárez said he had "intelligence and heart," was to become known as "father of the constitution of 1857." José María Mata, who later married the daughter of Ocampo (he met her in exile), was to be Mexico's Man in Washington and, later, minister of the treasury. Manuel Cepeda Peraza, a professional soldier turned liberal, was to play a role as governor of Yucatán. Juan Bautista Ceballos, though he had no great future, had been interim president between Arista's departure and Santa Anna's takeover. Ocampo, Arriaga, and Ceballos, in 1854, had the distinction of being accused by Santa Anna of organizing a "traitorous filibustering expedition" against Mexico—a crime they would doubtless have been happy to commit had they had the means to do so.

On the more personal side were José María Maza, Juárez' brother-in-law, who stuck with his friend Benito after having delivered doña Margarita's $400, and Pedro Santacilia, a young Cuban exiled by Spain. Pedro was to become Juárez' son-in-law, confidant, and trusted guardian of the family.

In New Orleans, these men and the rest of their group were nobodies. They depended for funds on what they picked up and on occasional lucky remittances. Ocampo helped discreetly until his money gave out (his estates were soon confiscated). To the Americans, they were not only down-at-heel foreigners but also recent enemies in war—hence, potential enemy aliens. All of them were probably "greasers" to the lower-class whites of New Orleans. Some of the more dark-skinned, notably Juárez, must often have been called "nigger." We know that he, for one, was subject to the black curfew. Undoubtedly, he suffered other discriminations.

When funds ran low, Mata worked as a waiter, Ocampo as a potter. Juárez and his brother-in-law, holed up in a ghetto flophouse run by a black woman, learned to roll cigars and cigarettes for a dubious tobacconist who doubled as a quack doctor. At night, the two took their products to suburban saloons and peddled them. On the proceeds, they drank *café au lait* and ate black bread at the market stalls. Sometimes, in the mornings, they fished. When fish were biting, calorie intake went up.

Luckily for Juárez, he not only had an indomitable will but also was strong as a horse. In late 1854, he was struck down by yellow fever and survived without medical care—let alone medicine as we know it. Once he got his health back, he devoted all the time he could to the study of the American political system. (Apparently, he read English fairly easily by now, though he never spoke it well.)

These brief glimpses of exile life in New Orleans are among those generally accepted as fact. There are many apocryphal tales as well. Whatever their personal lives, the expatriates held endless strategy councils; published manifestoes; badgered the local Mexican Cousul with representations; quarreled with each other, then made up; and, generally, rode their horses in all directions. It was a frustrating life. After a time, Ocampo moved with his daughter to the Texas border town of Brownsville, to keep in touch with rebel movements already afoot in northern Mexico. Others came and went. Juárez remained in New Orleans, studying constitutional law and keeping up with developments at home as best he could.

In Mexico, the wheels of revolution were beginning to move at last. The seeds of discontent, well watered by now, were putting forth shoots on every side.

Santa Anna's rule grew progressively harder to take. He built up his army to a 95,000-man instrument of repression, kept a tight rein on public utterance, and continued to exile what opposition he encountered. He was highly efficient at collecting taxes, but he spent the money like water. He borrowed at home and abroad at fantastic rates, while allowing his favorites to dip into the till. Bankruptcy was staved off for a while by the sale to the United States of a parcel of border land (the Gadsden Purchase) for $10 million. That money, too, was soon gone.

Meanwhile, pomp and ceremony flourished. Among other things, the dictator revived Iturbide's Order of Guadalupe. The citizenry got a good laugh when a sleeping partner of the night made off with the peerless leader's medals, then paraded the streets with the Grand Cross of the order gracing her bosom. The little man toyed with the idea of making himself emperor, but recalled the fate of Agustín I. He settled for the status of a prince-president, styling himself Serene Highness.

Rebellion had been brewing in the north, the center, and the south. In February, 1854, in the southern state of Guerrero, the shooting began. Juan Alvarez, a dark-skinned, hard-bitten guerrilla hero who had started his insurgency under Morelos, went into action. The Plan of Ayutla was proclaimed in the small town of that name. It called for a new president, preferably a rebel general, to rule until a new constitution could be drawn up. Various other states pronounced against the government.

High living had not dulled Santa Anna's instinct for self-preservation. Without further ado, he dashed down the road to Veracruz while it could still be held open. Pausing only long enough to make an announcement that he was turning back to the nation the powers it had entrusted to him "so as not to serve as a pretext for civil war," he caught the first boat for Havana.

The record is unclear as to just what role the New Orleans exiles played in formulating the Plan of Ayutla. Some claim they drafted it. Others say they merely adhered to it. It is known that Ignacio Comonfort, soon to become Alvarez' second-in-command and political adviser, stopped off in New Orleans on his way back from a successful trip to purchase Yankee arms for the rebels—and, also, that he maintained a full-time liaison man there. Doubtless the New Orleans group was in the act. Nonetheless, it was Comonfort, as Alvarez' man on the spot, who carried the executive responsibility for the plan.

For all his wooden-Indian façade, Juárez, during the pre-rebellion period, was on pins and needles for news. His letters were filled with rumors he had heard and conjectures as to what might be true, what false. Finally, in February, 1855, he made himself spokesman for the group in New Orleans and wrote Ocampo at Brownsville, urging that he and Ponciano Arriaga repair forthwith to Alvarez' headquarters in Acapulco. Ocampo and Arriaga agreed in principle, but deferred departure because the former was ill.

Comonfort, meanwhile, wrote Juárez directly, urging him to come head up the movement in Oaxaca. Juárez hesitated, out of deference to Ocampo. Comonfort then wrote Ocampo, begging him to send Juárez and, if possible, several others.

In Brownsville, Ocampo and Mata constituted themselves a revolutionary committee of two, raised a loan on the chances of a liberal takeover, and sent Juárez $250 passage money with their blessing. In due course, Juárez was to write:

I lived in that city [New Orleans] until June 20, 1855, when I left for Acapulco to offer my services in the campaigns that don Juan Alvarez and don Ignacio Comonfort were directing against the tyrannical power of don Antonio López de Santa Anna. I made the journey by way of Havana and the Isthmus of Panama, and I arrived at the port of Acapulco at the end of the month of July.

Exile was over. No matter what the future might hold, Benito Juárez was back among his people. Soon, God willing, he would be reunited with his beloved wife and family.

7

The Reformers

CHARACTERISTICALLY, JUÁREZ' bareboned account of the trip home makes no mention of its hardships. He arrived in Acapulco almost in rags. Also characteristic of Juárez is the story of how he joined General Juan Alvarez.

In Acapulco, he located Colonel Diego Alvarez, Juan's son, and asked to be taken to the General. The name of the nondescript, down-at-heels stranger, if indeed the Colonel caught it, rang no bell. He, himself, tells that Juárez, when asked what he wanted, simply said he had heard men were fighting for liberty and wanted to make himself useful. In any case, the younger Alvarez took Juárez to his father's camp. En route, they were drenched by a tropical downpour.

The old general got the bedraggled stranger some cotton pants and a blanket, but did not know what to make of him. He asked whether the stranger could read and write. The answer was yes, so Alvarez gave him a few simple letters to answer for his signature. This Juárez did "with the utmost modesty," and was taken on as a secretary. It was only some days later, when a letter from Ocampo addressed to "Lawyer don Benito Juárez" stimulated inquiries, that the Alvarezes realized they had a former governor on their staff. When Diego, "covered with embarrassment," asked Juárez why he had not said so, the answer was, "Why should I? What importance does that have?"

Juárez' modesty was typical of him, but it may also have reflected realization of his own position. During the weeks he had been at sea, the rebellion had grown from a chancy gamble to a near-sure thing. Juárez had left New Orleans as the chosen emissary of an important revolutionary element. By the time he got to Acapulco, he was virtually a fifth wheel. With great good sense, therefore, he quietly slipped into a political advisory role and did his usual effective job. It was not long before he had a chance to shine.

As soon as Santa Anna took off for Havana, his generals tried to jump onto the revolutionary bandwagon. They pronounced for the Plan of Ayutla, and named one of their number president to put it into effect. There was jubilation in Acapulco. Juárez was asked to write an article hailing the good news. It was only when he politely pointed out the obvious— that the Santa Annists were simply trying to save their skins— that young Alvarez and the other Acapulco innocents came to their senses.

The elder Alvarez, when he got word of the ploy, was no more taken in than had been Juárez. He gave the latter a seat on the board he named to receive—and reject—the propositions brought by emissaries of the Mexico City generals. He then started his march on the capital. En route, he paused to have himself elected president by a representative council picked from all the states. In mid-November, the old guerrilla campaigner, a mestizo, rode into Mexico City at the head of a colorful and fearsome-looking horde.

In Alvarez' cabinet, the top spot went to Melchor Ocampo, returned from exile. He was made minister of interior and of foreign affairs. The next most influential job, that of minister of war, went to Alvarez' chief political advisor and top general, Ignacio Comonfort. The poet Guillermo Prieto, a radical reformer who had been much in the public eye, was made minister of treasury. To Benito Juárez went the ministry of justice and public instruction.

During the period of developing resistance to Santa Anna, not all resistance fighters were doctrinaire liberals. The liberal camp became divided into *puros* and *moderados*, each group with its own degrees of left and right. The *puros*, or progressives, looked upon Ocampo as their spokesman. The moderates rallied under Comonfort, their natural leader by both temperament and political philosophy. The moderates served as a buffer between the *puros* and the die-hard conservatives—who, although politically out, made good use of moderate cover to stay in the game.

A power struggle soon developed between Ocampo and Comonfort. In a matter of weeks, Comonfort outjockeyed his rival, who resigned and retired to his estates. Not long thereafter, Prieto also resigned. Juárez stuck with it.

Ignacio Comonfort was an honest man, but a compromiser. He had fought Santa Anna with a will and had made a point of inviting the radical New Orleans exiles to return and help build a new government. He genuinely wanted reform, but shrank from drastic measures. Also, though he did not admit to it, he had a sneaking—almost servile—admiration for the clergy and the rich. The latter perceived this and played upon it.

Juan Alvarez, though a hero to the masses, did not last long as president. The "respectable" classes not only despised his common ways and near-illiteracy; they feared, or professed to fear, his barbaric backwoods soldiery roaming about town. A mean-spirited and deliberately cruel campaign was mounted to snub and ostracize the President, in public and in private. Meanwhile, the clergy began stirring up trouble in the provinces. These uprisings were portrayed to Alvarez as a threat of civil war.

Bitterly fed up, the old warrior agreed to step down in favor of Comonfort and to retire to his ranch. In doing so, Alvarez made it an express condition of his resignation that the legislation initiated during his brief tenure should be preserved inviolate. His reason: One of the most significant pieces of legislation in Mexico's history had just been put on the books. This was the Juárez Law, in reality a presidential decree, generally known in its Spanish form—*Ley Juárez.*

As the anti-Alvarez campaign neared a showdown, Juárez, as minister of justice, had been working feverishly to get his legislation drafted and cleared. The *Ley Juárez* abolished the judicial immunities *(fueros)* of clergy and military in the civil branch and eliminated all other special courts for these privileged classes. It put them, like everyone else, under jurisdiction of the civil courts and the common law—at least for civil offenses.

Juárez has been both blamed and praised—according to the source—for slipping his law through with the dexterity of a shell-game artist. He used no underhanded methods, but his timing was perfect. He knew that Comonfort had no stomach for the measure but, as a lip-service liberal, dared not openly oppose it. Having secured Alvarez' approval in principle, Juárez caught Comonfort at a harried moment and got him to approve the substance while waiving specific clearance of the draft itself. Then, at a time when Comonfort was out of town, Juárez had his draft taken up for discussion. The President had been informed of Comonfort's approval in substance, and he gave the law his imprimatur. The *Ley Juárez* was published by decree on November 23, 1855, shortly before Alvarez stepped down from office.

As Juárez freely admitted, the hastily drafted law had its loopholes. Many privileges of the clergy remained untouched. Those of the military were only whittled at. Yet the principle of all men's equality under the law had been established. The effect was electric.

It was a challenge flung at the privileged classes. The clergy took the challenge and poured on more pressure in the provinces. Manuel Doblado, the moderate Governor of

Guanajato, thought to help the cause by raising the ancient banner of *Religión y Fueros* ("Religion and Immunities"). On the very day he did so, however, Alvarez stepped down. The moderate leadership, having captured the government, quickly got word to Doblado to lay off.

In explaining the position to Doblado, they suddenly got a good look at themselves. With something of a shock, they realized to what extent they had been playing the game of the reaction. No true moderate wanted to set back the clock of liberal progress—and the *Ley Juárez* had become, overnight, the sign and symbol of that progress. Also, like it or not, they were stuck with it—thanks to Alvarez' condition. Even Doblado saw the light and became a stalwart of the progressive forces.

Juárez, until now, had stayed discreetly in the background. He resigned shortly after Alvarez did, to clear the deck for a cabinet reshuffle. But he had become an instant celebrity— admired or hated throughout the land—and could not be just let go. Comonfort asked him to return to Oaxaca as governor. Juárez accepted.

Whether or not the moderate leadership was relieved to get the now number one *puro* out of the capital, there was a job to be done in Oaxaca. The liberal General sent to take over for the government had been subverted by the clergy. Santa Anna holdovers were running the show.

Juárez, harking back to 1847, must have had a sense of "here we go again." He departed from Mexico City with a force of Oaxacan soldiers who had been stationed in the capital, made advance contact with political and military elements he could count on, and approached Oaxaca. By the time he reached the state border, in January, 1856, the rebels gave up and passed over the reins of power without resistance.

Benito Juárez and family were back in their beloved Oaxaca. When they reached their home suburb of Etla—whence don Benito had been whisked off to exile three years before—a large, cheering crowd was gathered to escort them all the way into the Statehouse. The Bishop of Oaxaca, with whom Juárez had worked before, officiated at the welcoming *Te Deum* prescribed by protocol and custom. Whatever ironic thoughts may have coursed through his mind, Juárez went solemnly through the motions. He had not yet severed his Catholic affiliation, though that time was soon to come.

For almost two years, until late 1857, the Governor stayed in office and devoted his energies to the welfare of the state and its people.

In the military branch, he had brought with him Comonfort's express authority to assume command of all state forces. Freewheeling generals had always been a problem for state governors. Juárez enlarged the national guard and, with imaginative foresight, set up classes in military science at the re-established Institute of Arts and Science. The idea was to enable promising liberal youth to qualify for commissions in the national guard so as to strengthen that body's loyalty. Among the promising young officers of the time was Porfirio Díaz, a Mixtec mestizo who had previously studied law briefly under Juárez.

For the rest, the Governor organized a state welfare department, to put assistance on a social-service rather than a church-charity basis; reorganized the college of advocates; founded a hospital and set up a board of health; put a stop to the anachronistic use of passports within the state; and, finally, established the mint he had been blocked from setting up before. This gave local mining a much-needed lift.

Meanwhile, in the nation's capital, the government was making progress in spite of itself. In 1856, the *Ley Juárez* sparked emulation in the *Ley Lerdo*, which forced the sale of church real estate not actually being put to religious use. In 1857, the nation got its new constitution.

Miguel Lerdo de Tejada was an intellectual aristocrat, successor to Prieto as minister of treasury. His *Ley Lerdo* was to the economic field what Juárez' was to the judicial. Together, they were twin bombshells of reform. The intent of the *Ley Lerdo* was not to confiscate, but to oblige the church to divest itself of its vast corporate holdings. This was to stimulate the economy, and, incidentally, generate transaction taxes. Poor Indians and mestizos were to buy plots at auction, thus making Mexico a nation of small landholders. Such was Lerdo's vision. Unfortunately, idealist theory did not work out in practice. Few of the poor could scrape up even the modest amounts required. Foreigners snapped up the bargains. Also—a serious oversight—no distinction was made between church lands proper and Indian communal lands under church control.

These failings were not to be noted for some time. Meanwhile, the new constitution became a reality. In accordance with the Plan of Ayutla, a constitutional congress had been convoked in early 1856. By February of 1857, the new charter was ready for ratification.

The constitution of 1857 was a step forward for democracy in Mexico. Almost all the delegates were liberals—*puros* and *moderados* of varying degree. Clergy and military were excluded. Few conservatives made the team. Yet, in the end, as in 1824, the civil power remained unemancipated from the church. The most hotly debated article—one designed specifically to eliminate religious intolerance and Catholic monopoly—had to be dropped. As a riposte, Ponciano Arriaga managed to get past the moderates an article giving the government nominal control of the church.

By this time, only avowed reactionaries were disputing the basic principles of the Juárez and Lerdo laws. These principles were firmly incorporated into the new charter. Their inclusion brought the church up in arms. The Pope brandished the sword of anathema. Any Catholic who signed the document would be excommunicated.

Some delegates did stay away from the signing ceremony for this reason. A dramatic ceremony, an act of liberal faith, nonetheless took place. First honors went to the aged and infirm dean of Mexican liberalism, Valentín Gómez Farías. The old man, leaning heavily on two disciples, quaveringly appended the first signature, then solemnly swore to defend and uphold the new constitution of the Mexican republic. Comonfort and some 100 other delegates did the same.

In Oaxaca, once the national constitution was published, Juárez lost no time in giving the state its own new charter. Elections were held, and Juárez was returned as governor—this time by direct vote of the people. He got over 90 per cent of that vote.

At the same time that he was reconstituting the state, Juárez was having a run-in with the church. It all started when one of the Governor's secretaries, picked to head a task force on the new state constitution, had to give up his regular office duties. Juárez, always a friend of the working clergy, picked a capable young priest to replace him. When the Bishop forbade this, the cleric opted for public service and left the priesthood.

The church then ordered one of its parish priests to deny the sacraments to a deceased village mayor, on the grounds that the mayor had refused to retract his oath of allegiance to the anathematized constitution. Juárez ordered the priest arrested, and so informed the Bishop. The letter, dated June 22, 1857, ends with the words: "God and Liberty."

A week later, when Juárez was to be sworn in for his new term as governor—with the customary *Te Deum* on the program of events—the cathedral canons barred the church doors and staged a lockout. If the Governor wished to enter, he must call on his police and use force. Juárez had been warned of what was up. He simply stayed away.

To all intents and purposes, he stayed away for good. As he explains in the *Notes* . . . , Juárez saw in this incident a good opportunity to make the break and do away with official participation by church authorities in civil ceremonials. The Governor made it clear: he had no objection to anyone's going to worship in a private capacity, but there was no obligation to do so officially. Thus, Benito Juárez finally extended his long-held belief in separation of church and state to a practical rule of conduct. (The rule was not inflexible. Juárez broke it himself, occasionally, in later years.)

In the capital, the situation was fluid and unstable. After the signing of the constitution, there were frequent cabinet reshufflings and political realignments. The *puros*, having lost the fight for a truly church-free constitution, were in eclipse— down but by no means out.

The national elections of 1857 returned Comonfort to the presidency by a comfortable margin. The electorate, however, reflected the general confusion of the times. They voted in an almost entirely moderate, middle-of-the-road congress. Yet at the same time, without hesitation—though by a close vote— they chose the author of the notorious *Ley Juárez* to be president of the Supreme Court. Under the new constitution, the chief justice post was elective—and it carried with it the vice presidency of the republic, first post in line of succession to the presidency.

In forming his new cabinet, Comonfort deferred to this indicator of public sentiment by taking in both Juárez and a Juárez disciple, Manuel Ruiz. Ruiz became minister of justice. Juárez became minister of interior—a post that made him, among other things, chief of the nation's police and responsible for maintaining public order. Although he had at first resisted nomination, Juárez decided that by taking the job he could best throw the force of his convictions behind the reform movement.

Thus, at age fifty-one, Benito Juárez strode once more onto the national stage, this time to stay. He did not take his family with him, possibly because he foresaw what, in fact, lay ahead—a very rough time indeed. Saying farewell to doña Margarita and the children, he climbed aboard the stagecoach for Mexico City. On November 2, 1857, he arrived there.

Benito Juárez, though he did not know it, was never to see his beloved Oaxaca again.

8

Civil War I: Losing Battles

BY THE time Juárez took over the vice presidency and interior ministry, the winds of change were very much to be felt. Soon after swearing to uphold and defend the constitution, Comonfort decided he could not govern under it. He resolved to reform it—by constitutional means if possible, by unconstitutional means if not.

The key figure in this anomalous situation was, of course, the compromiser, Comonfort himself. He hated being an excommunicate, yet he shrank from outright appeasement of the clerical party—a course bound to bring civil war. As a result, he dithered and vacillated. First, he half committed himself to a conspiracy to overthrow his own government. Then, when the plot began to surface prematurely—and was, in fact, denounced in congress—he tried to get his friend, the Interior Minister, to join it. Juárez, who had some idea of what was afoot but not very much, replied calmly: "Truly, I wish you good luck and much happiness . . . but I will not go with you."

Whether because he had an unclear picture of what was going on or whether out of a certain loyalty to Comonfort, Juárez, the Minister of Interior, did nothing that day. The next day, December 16, Comonfort decided to throw in his lot with the Plan of Tacubaya, named for the former palace of the

Archbishop, outside the city. The plan had been put together there by an ex-card sharp General Félix Zuloaga and was backed by the church-army element. In simplified terms, it called for Comonfort to make himself dictator and, as dictator, to repeal the constitution. That night, Zuloaga's troops entered the city, posted the Plan of Tacubaya in public places, and took over. Next morning, when Juárez arrived at his office, an armed reception committee awaited him. For December 17, 1857, the entry in his diary reads simply: "I was arrested in the Palace."

(It should be noted at this point that the *Notes for My Children* were apparently finished before their author left Oaxaca. From that time on, all we have from Juárez is a simple diary. Most of the entries are brief and factual.)

Juárez was kept under guard in a room at the palace. Comonfort, in a sort of stasis, sat in his office and twiddled his thumbs. This went on for weeks. Meanwhile, the liberals were not idle. Guillermo Prieto, Manuel Ruiz, and others still at large generated a flurry of communications with and among the governors of states surrounding the capital. The upshot was a league of ten governors, sworn to uphold the constitution and to recognize Juárez as constitutional president as soon as he should escape to any of their states.

Zuloaga's backers, meanwhile, grew impatient at Comonfort's inactivity. On January 11, 1858, they demanded his resignation. When he balked, Zuloaga's troops moved in from the edge of town and Zuloaga was sworn in as president by an *ad hoc* conclave of priests and generals.

Comonfort and his family were permitted to go into voluntary exile in New York. In a very personal sort of farewell manifesto, the outgoing President declared that he had often thought of resigning—and this in favor of his Vice President and constitutional successor. Almost his last act in office, on the day of Zuloaga's takeover, was an act of conscience. He secretly released his constitutional successor. Juárez stole away in the night with Manuel Ruiz, one jump ahead of Zuloaga's bully boys.

This was the first of a long series of cliff-hangers that were in store for the new constitutional President of Mexico. In the days that followed, according to Juárez' diary, he and Ruiz spent the nights sleeping in the fields. At a point some twenty miles north of Mexico City, they hopped a stagecoach for the nearby state capital of Querétaro. There, the church bells were already ringing out the town's adherence to Zuloaga's Plan of Tacubaya. Narrowly eluding capture, they made it to the next state capital, friendly Guanajuato, by January 18. On January 19, Benito Juárez calmly went through a ceremony inaugurating him as president of the Mexican republic.

His legal title rested on a constitution that had been overthrown. His power derived from the support of ten state governors—and from his own tough will. On declaring the government established, the new President issued a manifesto to the nation. He promised to abide by the laws and the constitution under which he had come to power. He asked for the help of the Mexican people and the protection of Divine Providence.

He certainly needed both. The first was possibly more problematical. The Mexican masses, hard-working but apathetic, were used to pulling in their heads as each successive wave of action and reaction charged over them. Could they be stimulated into entering the game themselves?

Juárez next named his refugee cabinet. Many of the liberal leaders had got the word and rendezvoused at Guanajuato, most of them after escapades similar to those of Ruiz and Juárez. The first cabinet was headed by Melchor Ocampo, who had dodged his provincial surveillance. The others were Ruiz and two more escapees from the capital, Guillermo Prieto and León Guzmán.

The lines were now drawn for the fight that had been brewing ever since the *Ley Juárez* was published in 1855. The Governor's league scraped together a force of some 7,000 men.

General Anastasio Parrodi, the former governor of Jalisco, who had played a leading role in organizing the league, was made commander-in-chief. Juárez was persuaded to move west and establish his headquarters at Guadalajara, capital of Jalisco. The War of the Reform, also known as the Three Years' War, was on.

Shortly after Juárez' party got to Guadalajara, they received the news that Parrodi's army had been badly beaten in battle nearby. According to Prieto, Juárez, on hearing this report, remarked casually: "Guillermo, our cock has lost a feather." The events of our prologue then began to unfold.

In it, the reader will recall, we left the President impassively facing a firing squad. Just as the command to fire was given, the bearded, bespectacled figure of Prieto leaped in front of Juárez and roared: "Down with those guns! Down with those guns! Brave men are not assassins!" He continued to rant at the firing squad until the tension broke. The soldiers, weeping, threw down their guns. Reaction was general, and extravagant. Even Juárez showed emotion.

By this time, it was known that the main body of Parrodi's defeated army was approaching Guadalajara. The mutineers were losing their nerve, and were only too happy to agree on a ransom price and make their getaway. Juárez' party was moved for the night to the residence of the Vice Consul of France—a German who had served as chief intermediary in the negotiations and who had scraped together the ransom money. Next day, the mutineers marched out of the city as agreed. That night, Benito Juárez made another brief entry in his diary: "On the 13th the Palace Guard mutinied and I was made prisoner by order of Landa, who headed the uprising. On the 15th I recovered my liberty."

The episode at Guadalajara soon had its sequel. With a large enemy force reported approaching the city, it was decided that the government had better hit the road once more, leaving Parrodi to defend the city. With a military escort of seventy or so, Juárez and his ministers left on horseback for Colima near the Pacific.

On the first day, they were attacked by that same Landa who had led the palace mutiny. The President's guard held off the attackers until dark, but they were hopelessly outnumbered. It was only a matter of time. Juárez proposed that his ministers escape during the night. He himself would remain. This was not unbecoming, he said, since they exercised no military command. He as president did. The ministers would have none of it. If he stayed, they stayed. Juárez saw their point and thanked them. The whole civilian party stole out under cover of night and made friendly territory by dawn. Another cliff-hanger.

These two episodes, known today to every Mexican schoolboy, quickly fleshed Juárez out and brought him into national focus. Until that time, although his name was well known through his law, Juárez as a person had been a shadowy, almost sinister figure to most Mexicans. Now, he and his ministers, all civilians, fired the national imagination and gave the liberal cause something it needed—heroes to brag about.

The presidential party pressed on, accepting food and shelter wherever they could, sometimes throwing their sleeping mats on the ground, until, on March 25, they reached Colima. There bad news awaited them. Parrodi and his army had surrendered at Guadalajara. With his forces now scattered to the four winds, Juárez named Santos Degollado, Ocampo's successor as governor of Michoacán, commander-in-chief. He gave this remarkable warrior-in-spite-of-himself broad powers to tax, organize armies, and carry on the fight.

Degollado was the archetype of the liberal civilian general. A one-time university rector, gentle, frail, and nearsighted, he lacked military science but made up for it by his ability to instill and maintain morale—especially among troops in adversity. The man was a veritable phoenix. Time after time, he lost battles and troops. Time after time, he bounced back, organized a new force, and went at it again.

At this point came a break for Juárez. Manuel Gutiérrez Zamora, Governor of Veracruz on the Atlantic coast, invited him to come set up his government there. Veracruz was not only a strong liberal redoubt, it was a major seaport, with the assets of its customs receipts and its control of supplies brought in from abroad. Also, the city was ringed by malaria-ridden lowlands, difficult terrain for an enemy approaching from the interior.

Leaving Degollado to get on with organizing a new army as best he could, Juárez and party left Colima on April 8 and made it down to the small west coast port of Manzanillo. In due course, they got passage on an American steamer bound for Panama and, in effect, reversed Juárez' 1855 route to Acapulco—across the isthmus to Havana to New Orleans, then down to Veracruz. With the war chest all but exhausted, they arrived on May 4. The twenty-one–gun presidential salute was fired from that same fortress of San Juan de Ulúa whence Juárez had been deported five years before.

By this time, the President's party had lived in each other's pockets for so long that they were like a family, with all the ups and downs of family life. They were also used to living from one day to the next, in somewhat the manner of troupers playing one-night stands in the boondocks. Juárez was undisputed head of the family, but he ruled with a light hand. There were even mild diversions and innocent merriment. When they were on the go, they went at it hard. When circumstances kept them immobilized, they relaxed and wrote letters.

Meanwhile, back in Oaxaca, doña Margarita was preparing to join her husband. At age thirty-two, with eight children ranging from teen-ager to babe-in-arms, this remarkable woman set out on the long and rugged trek to Veracruz. It was less than 200 miles as the crow flies, but she had to shun the high road, for fear of meeting enemies, and take the mountain trails that, even today, are barely passable. Apparently, she got together a flock of burros, saddlebags, and baskets, a small guard of armed and trusted mountain men—probably from San Pablo Guelatao—and slept in friendly peasant huts along the way. It was a feat to dismay strong men, let alone a woman with small children. There must have been many an anxious moment before the day when she turned up, tired but happy, at her goal on the sea—to the surprised delight of her husband, his friends, and the whole of Veracruz.

When hostilities began, the enemy held practically all the cards. To begin with, he had the capital. Possession of that was nine points of diplomatic law. The major European ambassadors and ministers recognized Zuloaga's regime on the spot. (Diplomats in the field, then, had that latitude.) The American Minister, John Forsyth, did not much like what Zuloaga stood for, but he had no intention of chasing after Juárez and becoming a "nomadic diplomat." Also, he had his fish to fry. He, too, recognized Zuloaga—as it turned out, temporarily.

Politically, the conservatives had only negative policies— principal among which was abolition of the Juárez and Lerdo laws. This policy, itself, rather backfired, since many rich Zuloaga backers had bought up bargains in church lands. Nonetheless, the Pope gave Zuloaga's cause his blessing, and the church soon found itself committed to sizable sums for his war chest.

Militarily, the conservatives took the offensive immediately. They had the tremendous advantage of an experienced professional army—trained officers, disciplined troops, good logistics. Zuloaga was himself a mediocre soldier, but he had good general-officer material. Outstanding were the dashing young Miguel Miramón, an aristocrat of French lineage, and the rawboned Indian, Tomás Mejía. Mejía was a brave and able soldier who believed with a simple, uncomplicated passion in the church and the old order (as, it might be noted, did a great number of his fellow Indians).

The liberals, who now styled themselves the "constitutionalists" (as opposed to the "rebels"), not only lacked military professionalism but despised militarism itself. Yet they had to learn, and learn they did—the hard way. One advantage they had: a tradition of guerrilla warfare handed down through generations of old insurgents. Although the conservatives won the pitched battles, they could not cover the conquered areas indefinitely. As soon as they pulled out, constitutionalist guerrillas filtered back in.

With his fluid forces roaming the countryside and living largely off the land, Juárez had his hands full preserving a semblance of central control from Veracruz on the coast. His first priority was to keep the troops more or less fed, paid, armed, and up to strength. Since funds were always short, much of this had to be delegated to governors and generals, who tended to be freewheelers and prima donnas.

Of less day-to-day urgency, but in many ways more difficult, was the task of giving the people a feeling that the men in Veracruz, with Benito Juárez at their head, were *their* leaders and had something to offer that was worth fighting for. On top of that, Juárez himself had the never-ending problem of cohesion and coordination—keeping his generals, ministers, and other key men out of each other's hair and working productively as a team.

In this, the President excelled. No superintellectual or military mastermind himself, his genius lay in bringing out the best in others and using it to best advantage. At Veracruz, he was always the Citizen President, unglamorous, devoid of heroics, but with a burning moral power that attracted and held the best liberal talent. Whenever the chips were down, Benito Juárez was boss.

Another problem ever hanging over Juárez was the threat of foreign intervention. He had constantly to conciliate, and at least keep neutral, the European powers to which Mexico was staggeringly in debt—principally Britain and France. Their representatives at Veracruz—usually naval rather than diplomatic—were nonetheless meddlesome for the fact that they did not recognize Juárez. They had always at their beck and call a transient assortment of warships at the ready in Veracruz harbor. In January, 1859, they staged a joint naval demonstration, threatening to shell the town unless arrears on the debt service were paid. Ocampo, as foreign minister, managed to buy them off by pledging a percentage of the customs receipts.

At the same time, as we shall see presently, the Juárez government was getting itself more and more involved in a large-scale deal with the United States.

The other side had troubles too. Zuloaga's rule, heavy-handed and clumsy, alienated more and more of his conservative backers. At the end of 1858, he was overthrown by one general, who was in turn unseated by another. In January, 1859, a third general—Miguel Miramón himself—took over the Mexico City regime, retaining command of the army at the same time.

In February, Miramón laid siege to Veracruz as expected. Also, as expected, he could not penetrate the strong natural and man-made defenses of the city. The foreign ships kept hands off. After a month, with the malaria season drawing near, he had to give up.

While Miramón was before Veracruz, Degollado managed to mount a counteroffensive and threaten the capital. The effort fell short, but it won the dubious advantage of producing martyrs for the liberal side. At Tacubaya, outside the capital, General Leonardo Márquez, the ruthless gangster-in-uniform who had defeated Degollado, butchered not only his prisoners but also the wounded in the hospital—and with them nurses and interns who had come from the city to minister to the casualties of both sides. This act of barbarism shocked the world. Márquez was henceforth tagged "the Tiger of Tacubaya."

Today's generations, accustomed to living under the threat of atomic holocaust and other refinements of modern civilization, should never underestimate the horrors of warfare 100 years ago—or 500, or 1,000. Men, usually untrained and poorly armed, were taken from their families and thrown into combat. If wounded, they often as not died. Women, children, and elders, left to carry on the work at home, were victimized just as brutally as they are in the so-called limited wars of today. Commerce was at a virtual standstill. Bandits roamed at will. Throughout the land, war was hell.

9

Civil War II: Winning a War

MIRAMÓN'S ARMIES continued to hold the upper hand throughout 1859. At the same time, however, Juárez and his ministers were busy launching a counteroffensive. This was not military but political. Yet it was just what was needed to make the people identify with the Veracruz leadership. It was the program of the reform laws. The first of a series of decrees was published on July 12, 1859, and nationalized all church property, excepting buildings actually in use for religious services or instruction. Unlike the half measures of the *Ley Lerdo*, the 1859 decree was confiscatory.

Other decrees followed in close succession: official separation of church and state; immediate suppression of monasteries, and, more gradually, nunneries; nationalization of cemeteries; establishment of a civil registry to take the control of births and marriages away from the church. Furthermore, a distinction was made between church lands proper and Indian communal lands under church control. This the *Ley Lerdo* had failed to do—a tragic mistake. After the war, the government took steps to restore some of these communal lands to the Indians who had held and worked them, but full restitution could never be made for this unwitting side effect of Lerdo's unrealistic law.

The guarantee of complete freedom of worship, keystone of

the whole reform structure, was not long in coming. This freedom, together with the separation of church and state, marked the high point of Juárez' long struggle with the church—a struggle not against religion or its practice but against religious monopoly and feudal privilege.

Thus, the 1859 decrees did emancipate the civil power, as the constitution of 1857 had not—and they were later incorporated into the constitution of 1917, which is in force today. Roman Catholicism is still by far the predominant religion in Mexico—especially in the backward areas—but all religions are now free to practice. Protestantism is represented by many and varied sects, and synagogues are not uncommon. No sects wear religious habit in public.

Juárez had an intraparty fight on his hands to prevent the reform laws from coming out too soon and from being too radically drafted. As it was, the timing of issuance was just right. At a moment when the fighting was going badly and morale sagging fast, the effect on the cause was electric. Publication of the laws rededicated the liberals in their faith and gave them something worthwhile to fight for.

Juárez' action in issuing his reform laws in mid-conflict might be likened to that of Lincoln a few years later, when he published the Emancipation Proclamation in the midst of *his* war. Lincoln's political goal was to preserve the Union; his ideological goal was to abolish slavery. Juárez' political goal was to preserve constitutional government, but liberal ideology demanded one ingredient the constitution did not provide— religious reform.

Not that the government got rich quick on the proceeds. The sale of church lands went slowly, with the church fighting every inch of the way. The purchasers got a better deal than the government did. Juárez made more enemies among the devout, to be sure, but the reasons were religious-emotional rather than economic. It is worth noting that not even Juárez' severest critics, then or now, have seriously accused him or his colleagues of profiteering on the sales.

We have noted that, when Zuloaga took over in the capital, he was recognized temporarily by the United States. President James Buchanan had covetous designs on more Mexican territory—particularly the territory of Lower California *(Baja California,* still Mexican today). He also wanted rail rights across the northwest corner of Mexico and a right-of-way across the Isthmus of Tehuantepec. (The isthmus is the narrow neck of southern Mexico.) Development of a right-of-way across it, with free ports at either end, could have provided the Atlantic-Pacific shortcut that was later to be gained through the Panama Canal.

Buchanan hoped to make a deal along these lines with Zuloaga's regime, but things went sour. He withdrew recognition and recalled the American Minister, Forsyth. He then cast his covetous eye toward Veracruz, and sent an advance man down to see how the land lay. Juárez had already sent Ocampo's son-in-law, José María Mata, to Washington to angle for U.S. recognition. Mata had seen Buchanan, and the question of a treaty had been very tentatively broached—after which the Mexican was left dangling for months.

The advance man's report on his talks with Juárez, Ocampo, and others was optimistic—overly so, as it turned out. Meanwhile, Miramón was besieging and bombarding Veracruz. On April 1, 1859, when the coast had cleared, Robert Milligan McLane landed there as Buchanan's minister to Mexico, empowered to do business with Juárez. The question of recognizing the regime at Veracruz, or not, was left to his discretion.

Five days after arrival, McLane did recognize the Juárez regime as the constitutional government of Mexico. On the sixth day, he presented his letters of credence to the President. On the seventh, he sat down with Foreign Minister Ocampo to talk business.

McLane, an amateur at diplomacy, had obviously been premature in granting recognition first, talking afterward. Ocampo was not nearly as come-hither as McLane had been led to expect by the fast-talking advance man. The Foreign Minister was adamant, and the President was right behind him. The Mexican side would not give up "a palm's width" of Mexican territory; 1848 had been enough.

McLane left for consultation in Washington. Meanwhile, the military situation was growing worse again. The commander in the north, Santiago Vidaurri, pulled his troops out of the war. Degollado in the center met with another crushing defeat. Juárez replaced him with Jesús González Ortega, an up-and-coming leader but something of a prima donna.

Nonetheless, McLane returned to Veracruz in November. On December 14, 1859, the highly controversial McLane-Ocampo Treaty was signed. According to its terms, the United States acquired a perpetual right-of-way across the isthmus and the right to police it. It also acquired railway rights across northwestern Mexico. In return, Mexico was to get $2 million in cash, plus $2 million in credit against the settlement of all outstanding American-citizen claims on it.

The outcry was loud and general. The Miramón regime protested at once. Many liberals protested as loudly. Most of those who cried the hardest were aware only of what concessions *had* been granted. Few knew of those that had been refused—principal among them the sale of any Mexican territory. Few realized the extent of the pressures—disaster after military disaster, bankruptcy, menacing big powers—under which Juárez, Ocampo, and the rest had been sweating when the President finally made the decision to take a chance—a gamble that the advantages to be gained from playing ball with the *gringo* would outweigh the disadvantages.

The last word was said in the U.S. Senate. The Northerners saw the deal as an invitation to carry slavery south of the border. Commerce and industry feared an opening to the competition of cheap labor. Both North and South feared entanglement in Mexico's family quarrel, and many regrettable things were said about the Mexicans as people. The McLane-Ocampo Treaty was not ratified.

Juárez could have lived with the treaty had he had to. He gave up no Mexican soil. Also, he trusted in the basic integrity of the American people. As things turned out, with the U.S. veto, he was not called upon to permit even a localized infringement of Mexican sovereignty. And the name of the game was U.S. recognition. This asset was to be turned to major advantage in the long run. In the short run, it paid off in a minor but very satisfying way.

What might be called the "Antón Lizardo caper" added a bit of lightness to the generally grim picture of the Veracruz period. It also vindicated, in some measure, Juárez' trust in the average American—in this case, the American sailor.

Miramón, despite his string of victories, was nigh bankrupt by the end of 1859. And when he destroyed one Juarist army, another popped up to take its place. He decided he must storm and capture the Juarist capital once and for all. With a sizable force he left Mexico City, and, at the end of February, 1860, set up his command post near Veracruz.

This time Miramón had an ace in the hole—or thought he had—in the form of a navy. Through agents, he had purchased two transports in Havana and had them fitted out by the Spaniards, well armed and loaded with munitions and supplies. Under the command of a Mexican officer, Tomás Marín, they were to blockade Veracruz harbor and force Juarist commerce to a port down the coast that Miramón planned to occupy.

The outfitting of the ships soon became an open secret in Mexico City. The American Consul there (a businessman) reported it to McLane, who informed Juárez. This was during the period when the McLane-Ocampo Treaty was awaiting ratification in the U.S. Senate.

Juárez declared the ships pirates—in advance. He further

chartered two small American steamers then in port, the *Indianola* and the *Wave*, and had them armed. The United States also had a fighting ship in port, the U.S.S. *Savannah*. Its instructions were simply to "protect the persons and property of citizens of the United States." The Captain of the *Savannah* made it clear that, unless U.S. interests were endangered, he would preserve strict neutrality.

Marín with his "two large steamers," instead of making unobtrusively for a spot down the coast, sailed brazenly into Veracruz harbor. Despite a warning shot from the harbor defense, he hoisted no flag. After communicating with a Spanish ship nearby, his two vessels stood down the coast "in the direction of Antón Lizardo."

Juárez immediately ordered the *Wave* and the *Indianola* to go after them. The senior American naval officer directed his second-in-command to follow in the *Savannah*. At Antón Lizardo, an encounter took place. The noise and the flashes could be heard and seen from Veracruz rooftops.

What followed was a confusion of who was doing what to whom, but after a running fight of almost two hours, Marín and his ships were captured. They were sent under escort of another American warship to New Orleans, where, in due course, a prize court ruled that Marín had committed no act of piracy. This was all very well, but Miramón had lost his support from the sea—not to say munitions and supplies—at the time he most needed it.

On March 21, after a withering bombardment of Veracruz that drove foreign residents aboard their ships and provoked British protests against the useless slaughter of civilians, Miramón raised the siege. Once again he straggled back to Mexico City, beset by guerrillas and desertions as he went. This was the turning point of the fighting war, and Miramón doubtless realized it.

If Miramón had his troubles, Juárez had plenty of his own. The bombardments of Veracruz had not helped. In the week before the siege was lifted, thirty-eight noncombatants, including women and children, were killed. Juárez sent Margarita and the family to the castle of San Juan de Ulúa, but he and his ministers stuck it out in town.

More serious to Juárez was a general decline of morale within the leadership. Over the past year, several of his generals had shown tendencies to negotiate independently with the enemy. In the cabinet, both Degollado and Miguel Lerdo (at the time, Foreign and Finance Minister, respectively) gave signs of losing their nerve. When Her Majesty's Government decided, in mid-March, 1860, to step in as mediator and put a stop to this war that interfered with British profit-taking, Lerdo and Degollado were all for it. Juárez was not.

Britain's opening proposal was for a six to twelve-month armistice while a nation-wide assembly drew up a new constitution. In the ensuing months, the British as go-betweens carried messages back and forth between Mexico City and Veracruz. The more defeatist of Juárez' ministers continued to urge a truce. The French tried to get into the act. The Spanish importuned in other ways. Against any trifling with the constitution, Juárez stood like a rock.

Since the day he had had the all-but-empty honor of the succession thrust upon him in 1858, Benito Juárez had come a long way. He was now, at the end of 1860, the very sign and symbol of constitutional government in a democratic and secular Mexico—not only at home but abroad. His ministers and generals wheeled and dealed, sometimes among themselves, sometimes with the other side, but, when they came up against *el Presidente*, they found out who was boss. Weathering all vicissitudes without losing his calm, making minor concessions but never losing his sense of direction, the rugged little Indian was to come out of Veracruz the undisputed head of a reform leadership forged and hardened in crisis after crisis.

After Miramón withdrew from Veracruz, it became

Manuel Doblado   Jesuś González Ortega

increasingly evident that things were looking up militarily. Miramón and his generals Mejía and Márquez won occasional battles during the course of 1860, but the smell of their defeat was in the air. Little by little, they were forced back on Mexico City. On August 10, the constitutionalists, under González Ortega, won their first major victory, at the town of Silao, some 180 miles north of the capital. Degollado was once more back with the troops. Manuel Doblado, the powerful but ego-ridden Governor of Guanajuato who had sat out the war since his defeat at that same Silao in 1858, came back in. A new general from the north, Ignacio Zaragoza, was making a name for himself. Troop morale—that ever imponderable element—was up and rising. To the Juarists, the smell of victory was in the air at last.

All did not go smoothly, however. Victory or no, there was a dearth of money. For some reason, neither side had resorted to the printing press. There was no fiat money. And both sides needed cash in the worst way.

In the fall of 1860, a constitutionalist general seized a mule convoy transporting silver ore from the mines and made off with more than $1 million belonging to foreigners, mostly British. Degollado made things worse by repaying almost half the take, then got involved in more freewheeling peace negotiations. Juárez relieved him of his command.

Later in the same year, Miramón authorized Márquez to break into Her Majesty's legation and appropriate some $700,000 of British bondholders' money. It was about this time that Britain, France, Spain, and Prussia began seriously to consider an alliance of intervention. The United States was approached but refused to have any part of it.

On the fighting front, Miramón made one last desperate throw. In a quick and masterly sortie out of the capital, he fell upon a large constitutionalist force and captured most of it— including not only its commander, Felipe Berriozábal, but also Santos Degollado, who after his dismissal had re-enlisted as an ordinary soldier. Meanwhile, Ortega's growing force approached the capital. On December 22, Miramón went to meet him at Calpulalpan, outside the city, and was crushingly defeated.

That was that. Miramón retreated to Mexico City and surrendered it to his prisoners, Berriozábal and Degollado. He divided what loot remained with his top accomplices, narrowly made it to the coast, and escaped to France in a French warship—much to the annoyance of the British, who wanted him for armed robbery of their legation. Márquez and the other rebel leaders took to the hills and to banditry.

On the night of December 23, 1860, President Juárez and his family, together with the Governor of Veracruz, were attending a performance of Bellini's opera *I Puritani*. In mid-show, a courier from Calpulalpan broke into the presidential box. Juárez scanned the message, got to his feet, and signaled the music to stop. The audience grew silent. In a low voice, the President read the bulletin aloud. A battle had been won. A war was over.

It was a great moment for Benito Juárez. As he stood there, looking like a bronze statue, silent and almost withdrawn, bedlam broke over him. Singers and orchestra swung spontaneously into *La Marseillaise*, all unconscious of its portent for Mexico. The crowd surged onto the street in ecstasy.

On New Year's Day, 1861, González Ortega entered the capital at the head of his troops. There was no looting. They were received with open arms. A heartwarming bit of byplay caught the public fancy and set the tone. As he rode at the head of his troops, Ortega caught sight of Santos Degollado watching from a balcony. Calling the old man down, he embraced him, handed him the flag, and set him at the head of the victory parade.

It took ten days for the President and his ministers to make it from Veracruz to the capital. On January 11, 1861, a plain little black carriage driven by Juárez' faithful coachman, Juan Udueta, entered Mexico City. In the carriage, erect and somber, sat Mexico's first citizen.

The welcome was tumultuous. With Ortega as master of ceremonies, the ovation went on for hours. Then Benito Juárez and his ministers got down to work. The treasury was empty; the economy was in chaos; the people were exhausted.

There was also a huge foreign debt outstanding. Although Juárez and Mexico did not then know it, in less than a year the nation would be called upon to defend its independence, its very existence, against the armed might of imperial France.

10

The Imperial Invader

ALTHOUGH THE War of the Reform had been won, peace brought little more than an end to the organized shooting. A ruined economy and hungry foreign creditors apart, disorder reigned internally. Governors and other politicians put egotism above patriotism. The press was irresponsible. Radicals screamed for vengeance on the vanquished.

For a time, even Juárez seemed indecisive in reacting to some of these problems. On one point, however, he stood firm. There would be no mass vengeance, no mob trials. At his first meeting with his ministers, it was decided to try certain top leaders of the rebellion on conspiracy charges, to expel as undesirable the Papal Legate and three of the most conniving diplomats—those of Spain, Ecuador, and Guatemala—and to banish the most activist of the bishops. For all others, amnesty.

Also, at the first working session of January 11, Juárez got going on new elections, both presidential and congressional. The necessary decrees, already set in motion over a year before, were published that same day. There were three candidates for president: Miguel Lerdo de Tejada, Jesús González Ortega, and Juárez himself. The author of the *Ley Lerdo* was to die before the elections took place, leaving Juárez and his successful general as sole contestants.

The problem of financing the government was an overwhelming one. Actual value received from the sale of church
lands was far below expectations. With production and
commerce disrupted, there was almost no taxable economy.
The federal share of collectible state taxes was minuscule, as,
indeed, it always had been. The government had to borrow
from usurers for such items as paying the police. Even so,
Juárez managed to reopen the schools and make a beginning on
the railroad to Veracruz.

Worst of all, the customs receipts, normally at least half the
federal income, were mortgaged in all but a small part to
Britain, France, and Spain. With the incubus of foreign debt
sucking up every source of reconstruction revenue, the
question arose: Why not a moratorium? "What," said a leading
daily about the foreign creditors, "will they gain by being
inexorable and by killing, so to speak, the goose that lays the
golden eggs?" The suggestion was put aside at the time, but it
was not forgotten.

Politically, 1861 was a year of trouble and passion. There
were frequent cabinet reshufflings. Many trusted revolutionary
figures tried their hand at one ministry or another. Juárez even
made that revolutionary of revolutionaries, Ignacio Ramírez,
minister of justice and public instruction. Ramírez, known as
"the magician," was a brilliant poet, journalist, law professor,
and a card-carrying atheist. He, Ocampo, and the brothers
Lerdo de Tejada were probably the best equipped intellectu-
ally of the liberal leaders.

Yet the government was under constant attack for a lack of
revolutionary zeal—not only by a radical youth forged in war
but also, of all things, by the moderate opposition. Juárez
himself bore the brunt of these attacks. In the eyes of his critics,
he had been bypassed by events and was no longer capable of
creative revolutionary activity.

As if political and economic troubles were not enough,
outlaw bands under Márquez, Zuloaga, and other rogues

roamed at will and exacted their toll in lives and treasure. In the year 1861, Mexico lost three outstanding sons to these conscienceless assassins.

First, Melchor Ocampo. In retirement on his estate, he was dragged from his house by gunmen, taken away to be shot, and left hanging from a pepper tree by a country road.

There was an immediate hue and cry for reprisals against the political prisoners awaiting trial in the capital. Juárez received an angry group demanding summary justice, but stood his ground firmly. As the leader of an enlightened society, he said, he would never permit the law of lynch against prisoners under the protection of the law of the land.

Young General Leandro Valle, standing athwart the prison gates, faced yet another crowd and "imposed his will on their frenzy." In less than a month, Valle went after the outlaw Márquez and was ambushed and murdered. Shortly before that, the officer and gentleman who was Santos Degollado met the same fate on a similar mission. Mexico and its leaders went into deep mourning.

Two months later, González Ortega cornered and defeated Márquez' guerrillas, but the slippery Márquez himself escaped. In this action, Colonel Porfirio Díaz distinguished himself. Ortega made him a general officer. Juárez himself confirmed the promotion.

With elections coming up, Juárez went before congress on May 9, 1861, to surrender the extraordinary powers he had inherited from Comonfort and ruled under since 1858. In so doing, he accepted responsibility for all his administration's measures that were "not in the strict bounds of the constitution." He then withdrew from the public eye, resolved not to lift a finger to influence the vote. He lived up to his resolve.

On June 11, the electorate returned Benito Juárez to the presidency. For all the recriminations, for all the accusations and attacks he had been subjected to, he was still the people's choice.

Nonetheless, though Juárez did win an absolute majority, the opposition managed, through a quibble, to have the election thrown into congress. Congress ratified the public's choice of Juárez, but only by a 61–55 vote. The lawmakers then took an unprecedented step—unconstitutional, in fact, since the choice belonged to the voters. They declared the runner-up, Jesús González Ortega, president of the Supreme Court. This put Ortega in the same position of succession to Juárez as Juárez had been vis-à-vis Comonfort.

The President's troubles did not end with re-election. The new congress was fractious. Clandestine support built up to replace Juárez with Ortega. In early September, things came to a head. Fifty-one deputies signed a petition urging Juárez to recognize he had passed his peak and resign for the good of the country. (If he had, of course, Ortega would have replaced him.) Then, sensing the will of the country, fifty-two other deputies drew up a strong statement of confidence in the President.

If his critics had thought to buffalo Benito Juárez into giving up in disgust, as others had, they woefully underestimated his iron nerve. Nobody beat Juárez in a war of nerves. Like an Old Testament prophet, he stood unshaken and unmoved—though not unforgiving. As was his nature, he held no grudge against his opponents. He did not even mention the 52–51 vote in his diary until he had occasion to allude to it some weeks later. Yet, strong though he was, within his Indian labyrinth of solitude, the ordeal must have told on him.

During these parlous times, a new source of strength arose to shore up the Juárez morale. The election campaign had seen some low-blow attempts at racism: Juárez was an Indian, hence, inherently inferior. Not only did the responsible press and public promptly cry foul; a group acting as spokesman for the Indian population testified in print to the pride it felt that "for the first time since our emancipation from Spain the majority of the inhabitants of Mexico, composed of its real natives, sees that its destinies will be governed by one of its blood brothers, that Mexico will be represented in the eyes of other states as it is, for Juárez is its very incarnation, for Juárez represents its virtues by his modesty, its craving for progress by the progressive laws he has issued, its love of the land by his pre-eminent patriotism."

Heartening as this must have been to Juárez, he never let his commitment to Indian betterment stand in the way of his responsibilities to the nation as a whole. And that nation, despite the outpourings of a vocal minority, now clearly stood behind him.

Meanwhile, in the north, Abraham Lincoln had been elected president. This was a break for Mexican-American relations. Before Lincoln took office, Juárez' new Minister to Washington, Matías Romero, called on him at his home in Illinois. Romero was a long-time protégé of Juárez' from Oaxaca days, and a stalwart of the reform. He also shared in the Guadalajara adventure of our prologue, and wrote an account of it.

Of his interview, Romero wrote Juárez that he had explained to Mr. Lincoln the causes of the war in Mexico—the efforts of clergy and army to retain their colonial privileges, the liberals' resolve to stop them. Lincoln had replied that "during his administration he would do everything in his power to favor the interests of Mexico, that it would be justly treated in every event that occurred, and that it would be considered a friendly and sister nation." Romero also briefed Lincoln on Mexico's antislavery orientation—which pleased him—and left several papers to be read at leisure. Two days later, Lincoln sent Romero a friendly note of acknowledgment.

For his part, Lincoln's choice of a diplomatic representative to Juárez clearly showed where Northern sympathies lay. Thomas Corwin of Ohio, aside from having had a distinguished public service career, had laid his political career on the line

> Springfield, Ill. Jan. 21. 1861
> Mr. Matias Romero ..
> My dear Sir,
>   Allow me to thank you
> for your polite call, as loharge of Af-
> fairs of Mexico— While, as yet
> I can do no official act on be-
> half of the United States, as one
> of its citizens, I tender the expression of my sincere
> wishes for the happiness, prosperity,
> and liberty of yourself, your govern-
> ment, and its people—
>   Your Obt. Servt
>   A. Lincoln

when, as a senator, he led the opposition to the war of 1846–48. Corwin presented his letters of credence on May 21, 1861, after the American Civil War had begun. He was welcomed with great warmth by Juárez. Although, under the circumstances, he could do little of material value for Mexico, Corwin was to prove of great moral help to Juárez and his cause during the trying times ahead.

A representative of the Confederacy soon showed up in Veracruz. The government ignored him, but could not ignore the threat he represented. This was the possibility of an alliance of the Confederacy with the Mexican Bourbons—and, later, with France as well.

By mid-1861, finances were *in extremis*. Since the time a debt moratorium had been suggested, it had been several times debated and rejected. In July, the project came up again. This time it was approved by Juárez and the cabinet. On July 17, it passed in congress by a secret vote of 112–4. Mexico would suspend payment on all foreign debts.

The French and British representatives refused, at first, to believe such a thing could happen. When they realized it had, in late July, the French broke diplomatic relations, and the British suspended theirs. Spain had no great financial claims against Mexico, but had many of its nationals in the country. It was, moreover, still smarting over the loss of its empire. In any case, the Spanish could not afford to be left out.

On October 31, 1861, Britain, France, and Spain put their signatures to an alliance of intervention, ostensibly to collect what was owed them. That was the purpose of the exercise as stated in the convention they signed. The parties pledged themselves not to seek any acquisition of territory or any "peculiar advantage," and not to interfere with Mexico's internal affairs.

The intervention soon brought forth loud howls in London. Among the first to raise the general alarm was Horace Greeley's London correspondent, the international exile Karl Marx. Writing in the *New York Herald-Tribune*, Marx proclaimed: "The contemplated intervention in Mexico by England, France, and Spain is, in my opinion, one of the most monstrous enterprises ever chronicled in international history."

Still, the British, apparently, only wanted their money and the chance to keep tabs on their partners in crime. The aims of Spain were suspect by nature, though they proved honorable after the fact. Napoleon III, by contrast, had no honorable intentions whatsoever.

The United States, also having claims against Mexico, was invited to join. Lincoln politely declined. He blandly noted his satisfaction that no internal intervention was intended, and went on to say that the United States, though it shunned alliances, cherished a lively interest in the "security, prosperity, and welfare" of its neighbor Mexico.

For a time, Juárez permitted himself to hope that the object of the intervention was indeed only fiscal. Nonetheless, keeping fingers crossed, he alerted all governors and took what steps he could to tighten the national defense. On December 15, congress voted him additional powers to deal with the crisis. On December 29, an advance contingent of 6,000 Spaniards landed in Veracruz from Havana. On January 6 and 7, 1862, some 2,500 French soldiers and 700 British marines also debarked.

Once again the chips were down. Mexico mobilized as best it could, though no war had been declared. Already many conservative ultras were showing signs of going over to the enemy. On January 17, and, more strongly, on January 25, Juárez issued successive decrees. These set the death penalty for foreigners conspiring against Mexican independence and for those Mexicans who aided them. The decree of January 25, 1862, was to be pointedly remembered some five years later.

The allied leaders attempted to negotiate with the Mexican authorities. The Mexicans turned a deaf ear until the allies asked a favor. With the malaria season drawing near, they requested permission to move their troops inland to higher and healthier ground. Juárez seized the occasion for a *quid pro quo:* such permission could be granted only after preliminary ground rules for negotiation had been worked out to Mexico's satisfaction.

The allies accepted this. Juárez named his then Foreign Minister, Manuel Doblado, to represent him. His price for an unopposed move to healthier ground was that the allied powers recognize his government as sovereign and pledge themselves to respect that sovereignty in any negotiations. The allies agreed, and moved their troops inland. Juárez, meanwhile, made further dispositions for defense.

Why was Juárez so accommodating? He could have placed his troops strategically at the exits from the port and let the allies stew in their own tropical juice—or, under great tactical disadvantage, fight their way out into a no man's land. The key was, apparently, negotiation on a level of equality, to which European powers were not accustomed to paying more than lip service. Juárez still had hopes of making his creditors understand about the goose and the eggs.

In any case, once they had agreed to negotiate as equals, the allies had to concert a position among themselves. It was at this point that the British and Spanish saw clearly what the French were up to. Napoleon was using debt collection only as a pretext for embarking on imperialist aggression. The allied commissioners met on April 9. The Frenchman, exasperated by what he considered the naive scruples of his partners, soon tipped his hand. The alliance was dissolved. The French were free to do as they pleased—but on their own.

Juárez was thus able, in effect, to make a separate peace with Britain and Spain. The British drove a hard financial bargain, as was their wont, then pulled out. Madrid was represented by a man who was most unusual for a Spaniard of his time—General Juan Prim y Prats, a noble and a Catalonian. Prim happened to be married to the niece of a prominent liberal and had personally favored the Mexican cause all along. He did not even stay to negotiate. His forces also pulled out, and an agreement was reached later on.

The French set up headquarters at Orizaba, eighty miles inland from Veracruz. They proclaimed their mission a peaceful one—but in the same breath had the effrontery to declare that the French flag was in Mexico to stay and would be attacked at great peril. They also set up a puppet Mexican government.

Meanwhile, Corwin in Mexico and Romero in Washington repeatedly warned the U.S. Government of Napoleon's designs. Secretary of State William Seward made it clear that the United States opposed the establishment of any monarchy on New World soil, but he was in no position to invoke the Monroe Doctrine. He protested directly to the French. They

blandly denied any imperialistic intentions. Corwin attempted
to get Mexico a $2 million loan. Lincoln realistically refused
even to submit the proposal to congress with French forces
already on Mexican soil. The North had troubles enough.

Juárez in crisis was Juárez in his element. In a clear and
vigorous proclamation, he dryly summarized developments,
then eloquently called upon the nation to defend itself. The
French kept bringing in reinforcements, and many Mexican
collaborationists joined them. On April 27, a French force
began to march towards Puebla, a city about halfway between
Veracruz and the capital. Juárez called upon his people: "We
must now prove to France and to the entire world that we are
worthy to be free. The moment has come to act."

Almost 5,000 Mexican troops, under the command of Ignacio
Zaragoza, rendezvoused at Puebla. Although the city had

Cinco de Mayo (the Battle of Puebla, 1862): in the foreground,
French Zouaves behind rows of maguey

always been a church-and-privilege stronghold, its topography and its two well-placed forts made it relatively easy to defend. Also, as Zaragoza perceived, the French would be running low on supplies by the time they reached the city and could not afford to bypass it.

According to Zaragoza's report after the battle: "The French army fought with much gallantry; its commander-in-chief behaved stupidly in his attack." When the French charged in force across the sandy plains, the Mexican cavalry was concealed in ditches and behind rows of the tall cactus called maguey—a common plant of many uses (it is woven, eaten, distilled, used to hide behind, and so forth). The French, with their firepower and superior numbers, came within an ace of taking the forts by storm, but were temporarily thrown back. In the confusion, Porfirio Díaz audaciously pressed after them and got them on the run before they could discover how thinly spread his cavalry was. The French retreated from the field and made for their base at Orizaba, to await more reinforcements from France. They had taken some 500 casualties, twice as many as the Mexicans.

On May 5, 1862, Benito Juárez noted in his diary: "Received by telegraph a report that the French have been defeated." Then he, along with all of Mexico, gave way to a fierce, proud joy. No matter what the morrow might hold, today the ragtag little army of Mexico had beaten the greatest military power in the world. May 5, the *Cinco de Mayo*, is one of Mexico's most celebrated national days.

Of course, it could not last. Even in the euphoria of the victory celebrations, no one really expected it to. Benito Juárez' faith in Mexico and Mexico's faith in Benito Juárez were in for a long, hard time of blood, sweat, and tears before the final victory could be won. Juárez' plain little black carriage was soon to begin its long trek over the highroads and byroads of Mexico—always just one jump ahead of the invader.

11

The Imperial Pawn

BEFORE BEGINNING the story of Maximilian and Charlotte (later Carlota), let us take a brief look at its antecedents. The idea of a monarchy in Mexico had been played with in Europe since the late eighteenth century. In 1821, shortly before Iturbide seized power, an unauthorized delegation of Mexican royalists offered the crown to an Austrian archduke. Among them was a young man named José María Gutiérrez de Estrada, who, thus, began what was to be a lifetime career as Mexico's number one monarchist. Exiled in 1840, he married a rich Austrian countess and rode his royalist hobby-horse about Europe.

Associated at times with Estrada were José Manuel ("Pepe") Hidalgo, a social butterfly who was no relation to the great Hidalgo, and Juan Nepomuceno Almonte, reputedly an illegitimate son of the great Morelos. It was Almonte, back in Mexico as a camp follower of the invasion, who was named to head the puppet Mexican regime set up by the French in Orizaba. Two clerics filled out the expatriate monarchist leadership. Archbishop Pelagio Antonio Labastida, banished from Puebla, was an honest man who supported the project in order to re-establish the church in Mexico. Father Francisco

Javier Miranda was not an honest man but a schemer. He was a die-hard anti-Juárez ultra, and only incidentally a priest.

These plotters, individually or in combination with or against one another, peddled Mexican monarchy about Europe. By 1860, they had sold Napoleon III and the fanatically Catholic Empress Eugénie on it. These two, and especially Eugénie, were not at all averse to setting up and controlling a Latin Catholic empire in the New World. Napoleon's chief interest, however, was financial. Aside from the matter of the debt, he wanted to get control of Mexico's natural wealth—of which he had an exaggerated idea. Behind all this, it seems, the nephew of Napoleon I cherished an ambition to make it for once on his own.

To make his power play, the Emperor needed a pawn, a front man who was expendable—though, of course, he did not put it in exactly those terms. Gutiérrez de Estrada pointed him toward the Archduke Maximilian of Austria, younger brother of the Emperor Franz Josef. The choice had its advantages for Napoleon. A showdown between France and Prussia was already in the cards, and it would not hurt to have the House of Habsburg on his side. Maximilian was an imposing young figure of a man, and he looked every inch an emperor. Also, Napoleon knew, the Archduke was not very bright.

Maximilian and his young wife Charlotte, daughter of the King of the Belgians, were virtually unemployed in their gilded palace of Miramar, overlooking the Adriatic. Maximilian was a romantic dilettante and a charmer. A dabbler in liberalism who had even talked with socialists, he had ideas that, for a Habsburg, were no less than do-gooder heresy. Charlotte was comely and well trained, but strong-willed and driven by ambition. Both were ignorant of the world, self-centered, and hungry for the unreaped honors they considered their right as Habsburgs. For all the mawkish sentiment that has been expended on the tragic pair, they were, in fact, the victims not only of Napoleon but also of their own unthinking greed and wishful self-delusion.

They were *not* the victims of Benito Juárez, so often portrayed as Maximilian's implacable executioner. Georges Clemenceau, then an impatient young tiger of twenty-six, put it well in decrying the general pity for Maximilian under sentence of death. "To pity the wolf," he said, "is to commit a crime against the lamb."

As early as October, 1861, Estrada, with Napoleon's permission, first approached Maximilian. The Archduke, already aware of what was afoot, made three conditions for accepting the crown: he must have the permission of his brother Franz Josef; he must be assured of the military support of both France and England; and he must be offered the crown by the Mexican people themselves.

While steps were being taken to meet these conditions, Maximilian did not lack for warning that all was not sweetness and light. Archbishop Labastida did not like it. The Pope insisted on full restoration of the pre-reform church, manifestly impossible by this time. King Leopold I, Charlotte's father and Queen Victoria's uncle, insisted on a firm commitment of British support—but before the business had got off the ground, the British pulled out of Mexico. Finally, Maximilian was twice warned by a European agent of Juárez' that he would get cold welcome in Mexico. Maximilian remained confident that he could win "his people" over. He meant to support Juárez' reforms, and he had no intention of imposing himself on the Mexicans against their will.

Another warning, probably inaudible in the courts of Europe, was sounded in Washington. When asked: "Mr. President, how about the French army in Mexico?" Abraham Lincoln replied:

I'm not exactly "skeered," but I don't like the looks of the thing. . . . If we get well out of our present difficulties and restore the Union, I propose to notify Louis Napoleon that it is about time to take his army out of Mexico. When that army is gone, the Mexicans will take care of Maximilian.

In mid-1863, under French management, a handpicked Mexican assembly proclaimed the Empire. A delegation headed by Estrada, Pepe Hidalgo, and Father Miranda went to Miramar. Maximilian accepted the crown provisionally, pending an invitation from the Mexican people. (By this time, the condition of British support had been dropped.)

Almonte, in Mexico, took on the job of stimulating the spontaneous request for Maximilian's services. At the head of a three-man "regency" set up by the French, he carefully rigged a series of plebiscites in selected areas. When he had what seemed like enough returns, an overwhelming "yes" was reported to Maximilian and Charlotte in Miramar. By this time, if these two believed it was real, they were the only players in the game who did.

Maximilian did not accept on the spot, though it was a foregone conclusion he would. Napoleon and Eugénie took the lead in putting on a round of festivities for the highborn couple. The Emperor, meanwhile, conned the Archduke into signing a usurious convention concerning the status and payment of the French forces. Napoleon's troops were to be gradually phased out and replaced through a program of Mexicanization. Meanwhile, Maximilian (the Mexican people, that is) would pay for the cost of the French army. Napoleon, for his part, solemnly promised—though not in writing—never to desert Maximilian.

The Emperor-to-be then proceeded to England, where he borrowed at exorbitant rates and disregarded more advice to pull out before it was too late. Finally, back in Austria to pack, he and Charlotte were dealt a staggering blow by Franz Josef. The Emperor demanded that his brother renounce all claims to the Austrian throne, for himself and his heirs. Maximilian had been almost subconsciously holding that in reserve as an anchor to windward, in case something went wrong in Mexico. Now it was too late to turn back. Maximilian signed.

On April 10, 1864, Maximilian formally and unreservedly accepted the Mexican crown. Four days later, he and Charlotte sailed from Miramar aboard an Austrian frigate. They first stopped over in Rome and got the Pope's blessing—though there was no softening of his hard-line position on restoring the Mexican church. During the long crossing, the royal passenger addressed himself to two principal tasks. He spent most of his waking hours on what was to be, typically, his magnum opus: a complete manual on court protocol, precedence, and formalities. He also—believe it or not—composed a letter to Benito Juárez, proposing that they meet to talk things over and try to reach an amicable settlement of their differences.

On May 28, the golden couple arrived in Veracruz. Meanwhile, "somewhere in Mexico," a small, dark-skinned Indian looked quizzically at a report on their doings, sent by the European agent who had warned Maximilian about his reception. On the margin of the report, the President of Mexico made a seven-word annotation: "Letter from Zerman containing some curious news."

By the time the royal pair had set foot on Mexican soil, Juárez had moved his government three times. The little black carriage, often an office on wheels, moved further north each time.

By May, 1863, a little more than a year after the great victory at Puebla, the city had been encircled by the French and it was being slowly starved. It is said that the defenders were reduced to eating dogs and cats, even leaves and bark. Ignacio Comonfort (who had been taken back, pardoned, and given a command) tried to get a supply train through, but was jumped en route and badly beaten. Several months later, he himself was caught by the imperialists and killed.

By mid-May, González Ortega and the defenders of Puebla

ran out of ammunition, destroyed their weapons, and surrendered. The Mexican general officers refused to give an oath to stay out of the war and were sent to Veracruz for transfer to France. Porfirio Díaz, ever fertile in expedient, donned a plaid cape and walked out of jail with some of the friends and relatives who had been allowed to come say farewell. As he passed the gate, he locked eyeballs with a French officer who had once been *his* prisoner, saluted him without thinking, then came to his senses and beat it up the street. The Frenchman did a slow double-take, then rushed in to check the cells for Díaz. Too late.

By the end of May, Juárez accepted the inevitable. With only 14,000 men left under arms, with very little in the war chest, and with the French approaching the capital, the President agreed with congress that discretion was the better part of valor. The forces must be husbanded, built up for renewed resistance later. The government was to move some 250 miles north, to San Luis Potosí, and carry on from there. Once again, congress voted Juárez extraordinary powers. On May 27, 1863, he proclaimed:

> Great has been the reverse that we have suffered, but greater are our constancy and resolution, and we shall fight on with greater ardor, and with the certainty that victory will be ours, no matter what may be the elements on which the enemy can count, because the nation still has life, and strong sons to defend her.

The sentiment, if not the strung-out Spanish construction, would have done credit to a Churchill.

Four days later, at sundown, Juárez stood on his balcony as the flag was lowered. The troops presented arms. The national anthem was played. The flag was handed to the President, with ceremony. He pressed it to his lips, then cried: *"Viva México!"* The crowd roared it back, defiantly. That night, a little black carriage carrying the President, followed by a mule cart carrying the constitution and the national archives, led a small file of other carriages north.

As Benito Juárez rode in silence, hands on his straight black cane, his thoughts may have turned with some comfort to the recent declaration of a great French exile. Victor Hugo, passionate friend of liberty and passionate foe of Napoleon, had come out loud and clear for Mexico. It was the Empire that was fighting the Mexicans, he said—not France.

Nine days later, the President's flag was raised in San Luis. The next day, June 10, the French forces rode into Mexico City, accompanied by their leading Mexican jackals. Flowers paid for and distributed by France were dutifully tossed at the troops by the curious who had come to see the parade.

The move out of the capital signaled decentralization of the war. From now on, the battle field was all Mexico, and the army was all the Mexican people, excepting the traitors. As Juárez put it, "By reconcentrating in one point the enemy will be weak in all others and, dispersed, will be weak everywhere. He will be obliged to recognize that the republic is not confined to Mexico City or Puebla." Brave words and true—but the truth was promise, not yet reality.

San Luis Potosí, a neat little city nestling among the heights of the Sierra Madre, was probably even prettier then than it is today. For a time, Juárez was able to keep his beloved family with him. By November, however, the enemy was getting dangerously close. With a sigh, he packed Margarita and the brood off to Saltillo, another mountain city 250 miles north. This time, they went in the care of capable Pedro Santacilia, Juárez' young Cuban friend from New Orleans exile days. Pedro had recently joined the family by marrying Manuela, eldest daughter of Benito and Margarita.

San Luis, in many ways, was Veracruz, 1859, all over again. Juárez had constantly to solve problems and arbitrate squabbles. His key men took to freewheeling and generally behaving like prima donnas. Militarily, the situation was never

Maximilian   Carlota

quite hopeless but it was never good. The Juarists had to be careful, above all, not to be caught in pitched battles.

The enemy advanced steadily and inexorably northward. By the end of December, San Luis had to be evacuated. On January 9, 1864, Juárez set up headquarters in Saltillo, with the peaks of the Sierra Madre again looming nearby.

Five days after arrival, emissaries appeared from nearby Zacatecas in representation of Manuel Doblado, Jesús González Ortega, and an ex-governor named José María Chávez. It had been reported that the President was very fatigued and would be glad of a chance to retire. If this was true, the trio would understand perfectly and act accordingly. If it was not true, they would respect his decision to remain in office.

Once again, the pressure to resign—and, once again, in favor of Ortega. The little Indian must have thought to himself: "Oh no, not again!" To the emissaries, he simply said the gentlemen were mistaken. He had no wish nor any plans to resign, because, as he later reported himself as saying, "in the present circumstances, in which power had no attraction, neither my honor nor my duty permitted me to abandon the power with which the nation had entrusted me." He went on to note that he was as encouraged and determined as he had been six years before, and that, when he assumed command, he had foreseen the reverses and disasters that would be the natural consequences of such a struggle. They did not terrify him.

Juárez' decision was accepted. Doblado soon joined him with 1,500 men and four cannon. By now a more troublesome showdown was looming. In nearby Monterrey, metropolis of the north, Governor Santiago Vidaurri had become progressively more arrogant and more independent. Since 1858, he had played the summer soldier. He had traded with the Confederacy and dickered with the French. For all that he corresponded with Juárez in warm and polished prose, he was not refusing the federal government any share, whatsoever, of his state's taxes. His state included Saltillo.

Juárez decided to go to Monterrey and have it out. He started on the seventy-five-mile trip through the mountains with Doblado's 1,500 men and was joined, en route, by 2,000 men under General Florencio Antillón.

The confrontation was a washout for Juárez. To begin with, Doblado let himself be gulled into sending his four guns into the city ahead of him, for use in saluting the President's arrival. Vidaurri seized them. A scheduled midday meeting in town did not come off. Juárez occupied the Statehouse, downtown. Vidaurri stayed in the Citadel, a fortress on the edge of town. He protested his loyalty but refused to come downtown and talk until Juárez' troops had withdrawn. To avoid what appeared a certain armed clash, Juárez agreed.

Vidaurri then came to the Statehouse to meet Juárez, bringing with him a cheering mob of supernumeraries. He made unacceptable demands. Before long, weapons were seen to come out of Vidaurrist pockets. Juárez and party did a dignified quickstep to their carriage, which had been waiting like a getaway car. Their armed escort held off the indecisive mob as they made it out of town. ("At a trot," ordered Juárez. "The President of the republic cannot run.")

Vidaurri's contumacy was, at least, now in the open. Rashly, he held what he called a plebiscite. The choice, as stated, was between peace (go with the French) and war (go with Juárez). The few votes that were cast were heavily for "war." Juárez declared Vidaurri a traitor. Since the Juarist forces numbered 7,000 by now, Vidaurri fled to Texas. Juárez had won the showdown, but at the cost of time and effort that had better been expended against the invader. Also, it brought on the second illness ever to make a dent in the iron Indian constitution—what, in those days, was called "a bilious fever."

During this time, a bizarre little sideshow played itself out in Veracruz. Who should pop up from Havana but the great Santa Anna! The old fraud hoped to get in on the ground floor with Maximilian and had wangled permission to enter the country as a "simple citizen." Santa Anna a simple citizen? Impossible. Almost as soon as he hit dry land, the glorious leader started giving out Santannesque pronouncements. The French promptly redeported him.

The old boy eventually found his way to the States, where he tried without success to organize an anti-French expeditionary force to Mexico. While living in New Jersey, he managed to make one final—and lasting—bit of mischief. A young neighbor saw Santa Anna chewing something and asked what it was. It was chicle, from Yucatán. The young man's name was Adams. He got enough information from his neighbor to import, produce, and introduce the first American chewing gum.

By the time Maximilian reached Veracruz in late May, 1864, Juárez had his government well established in Monterrey. It was there that the invitation Maximilian had composed on shipboard reached him. Juárez regretted.

On June 13, Antonio, the Juárezes' twelfth and last child, was born in Saltillo. As soon as doña Margarita was able to travel, she brought the whole family to Monterrey. On July 12, Pedro and Manuela Santacilia presented Benito and Margarita with their first grandchild.

While the American House and Senate passed periodic resolutions condemning the French intervention, the French and their Mexican accomplices moved steadily north. Doblado's forces got caught out by Mexican imperialists at Matehuala, north of San Luis Potosí—a grievous blow. Juárez made plans for the defense of Saltillo and Monterrey.

He also, finally, made the reluctant decision to send his family to safe haven in the States. Just before Margarita's expeditionary force was to take off, the President bought his lady a going-away present—a beautiful brocade dress. He then accompanied the party to a little village outside Monterrey. There, with Santacilia in charge and with a small escort to take them as far as the border, the loved ones of Benito Juárez disappeared into the north—for how long, God only knew. On August 12, 1864, a forlorn little entry appeared in Juárez' diary: "The family left for Matamoros."

By this time, the French presence was making itself very much felt in the north. (The remains of their considerable fortifications may still be seen today.) The Juarist forces in Monterrey were already withdrawing to Saltillo, and some to points farther west. On August 14, the government announced it would leave for Saltillo the following day. When opportune, it would announce the place in which it would "continue sustaining the laws of the nation." That place was to be Chihuahua, some 400 miles to the northwest.

In the two months before Juárez got there, the little black carriage took quite a buffeting. Almost at the outset it was riddled by bandits' bullets. On their travels, Juárez and his

ministers were often short of food and water. They were,
however, almost always warmly received along the way. Their
procession was a retreat, not a rout. They often stopped for a
time to meet and consult with local politicos and generals,
though the news was seldom good. Soon after the trip began,
the weighty and voluminous national archives were entrusted
to eight good men, secreted in a mountain cave, and put under
continuous guard. It was to be three long years before they
could be given back.

The reign of Maximilian and Carlota (they were called
Maximiliano and Carlota by the Mexicans—and Carlota has
stuck to her) began on a series of small, sour notes. The
reception committee was late getting to the dock, and when
they did arrive, the royal couple had to be whisked through
hostile Veracruz—while the people pointedly ignored their
presence. The ornate imperial coach broke down on the rough
road to Mexico City. In the barnlike National Palace,
abandoned by Juárez, their quarters were unswept and
verminous.

Yet, they soon renovated the hilltop castle of Chapultepec on
the edge of the city, set to work teaching manners and protocol,
gave large and magnificent parties, and began making
grandiose plans for the betterment of the realm. They worked
on their Spanish and affected Mexican dress. Even more than in
Europe, they lived in a world apart. Such was their capacity for
self-delusion that, for a while, the couple felt happy and
accepted.

Discord soon appeared. Maximilian showed himself far too
liberal for French and Catholic tastes. He had difficulty
reaching a *modus vivendi* with Marshal Achille Bazaine, the
French commander-in-chief who was, in effect, his keeper. On
top of that, strain developed between Maximilian and Carlota.
She was both headstrong and neurotic. Her failure to produce
an heir did not improve matters.

The French continued to win pitched battles whenever they

could find them, but they could not keep their troops everywhere. As Juárez had predicted, they were spread too thin. The serpent on the Mexican coat of arms became a hydra. When the invader cut one head off, two more grew back.

Always a nuisance to Bazaine was Porfirio Díaz, who managed throughout 1864 to keep a Oaxaca-based force in the field. With the northern cities subdued, Bazaine tried to buy Díaz off and got laughed at. This irritated him into moving against Oaxaca in force. Finally, in early 1865, Díaz had to surrender, and became Bazaine's prisoner. Not for long. Having again refused to give his oath not to escape, "our Porfirio" pulled another Houdini and did so. Starting again from scratch, he was soon back in business as Bazaine's most-wanted guerrilla.

Through all this period, it might be noted, old Juan Alvarez was still in possession of the port of Acapulco, and he was keeping it open for shipments of arms bought in the States. He lasted out the war, then died at the age of seventy-seven.

During 1865, Bazaine grew overconfident and sent some of his troops home. He replaced them with Austrian and Belgian volunteers, soon to prove inferior. Even more remiss of Bazaine was his unwillingness to get on with the Mexicanization of his forces. He had, by this time, enough turncoat talent and manpower for the purpose, but he resisted any program of training or delegation.

Maximilian, meanwhile, progressed from minor errors to major blunders. When the Papal Nuncio demanded full rehabilitation of the pre-reform church, the mixed-up idealist who called himself emperor not only refused, but went so far as to confirm the Juárez laws on the subject. That did it. With one decree, Maximilian alienated the clergy, the Mexican Bourbons, and the Empress Eugénie—while gaining no liberal support in return. As Juárez remarked, Maximilian must be naive, indeed, if he thought to win over the Mexican people by adopting reforms already in effect. It was not their laws, but their independence and their national dignity, that Mexicans were fighting for.

Of Maximilian's literally fatal blunder, his 1865 decree ordering summary execution of all those caught bearing arms against the Empire, more will be said later.

Juárez arrived in Chihuahua on October 12, 1864. More trouble. Word awaited him that González Ortega, through atrocious generalship, had been defeated by a smaller French force in the adjoining state of Durango. Juárez and his ministers were, nonetheless, warmly received in Chihuahua, and they set up headquarters in the Statehouse.

At this time, his key colleagues were three: Guillermo Prieto, José María Iglesias, and Sebastián Lerdo de Tejada. Iglesias had for some time headed the Treasury. Sebastián Lerdo, brother of Miguel and a long-time university rector, had served as foreign minister almost since the beginning of the Juárez hegira in 1863. Isolated from their main forces, all of them did a lot of letter-writing. In one letter, Juárez wrote: "This Chihuahua is a jail in which one is held rigorously incommunicado, but not distant is the day on which we shall open our way into the interior with bayonets."

The period was a tragic time for Juárez personally. His second son, Pepe, died in New York, and, although the father did not get the news for a month after the event, his letters of January, 1865, show that he had an agonizing premonition that the youth was far worse off than first reported. The following September, his youngest boy, born only a year before, also died. Grief for his children was bad enough, but worry over Margarita was even worse. "I imagine all that my poor wife is suffering, I greatly fear that she will not be able to endure this blow, and this almost deprives me of any judgment. . . . My mind is overwhelmed, and I can hardly write these lines."

Juárez in Chihuahua was hanging on for the break. On April 9, 1865, it came. Grant took Lee's surrender at Appomattox. Joy over this event was soon turned to sadness by the death of

Abraham Lincoln. On May 11, Juárez wrote Romero from Chihuahua with instructions to call on Secretary Seward and, in Juárez' name, express his grief at the assassination of Mr. Lincoln, "who worked with so much earnestness and abnegation for the cause of nationality and freedom." In a letter of the same date to Pedro Santacilia, he expressed hope that Lincoln's successor, Andrew Johnson, would be "favorable to our cause."

Johnson was. The French got the wind up, fearing that the Union army might even move to the attack in Mexico. There was quite a bit of volunteering at the Mexican legation in Washington, and a few Americans actually got across the frontier and into action. There was moral, and often material, support all along the border. Gun-running, which, of course, had been going on all along, now became popular and easy. On the diplomatic front, Secretary Seward began issuing increasingly pointed pronouncements to the effect of: "Frenchie, go home!"

But Frenchie still had quite a sting in his tail. In July, 1865, he began to advance on Chihuahua. The American Consul in that city, Reuben W. Creel, reported: "The President is calm and inflexible, and says that the French can never get him to leave Mexican soil." On August 5, the little black carriage made one more trip north—this time to literally the last ditch, the narrow stream that separates Mexico from Texas. At El Paso del Norte (now called Ciudad Juárez), the President took his stand. He never did leave Mexican soil, though the Americans urged him to cross over if ever he needed to. A correspondent in Acapulco, asked where Juárez was and whether he would flee across the border, replied:

> It would be easier for the earth to move from its axis than that man from the Republic. . . . I do not know the name of the bit of earth where he is just now, but he is in the Republic, he works for the Republic, and he will die in the Republic, and if only a corner of the country remains, in that corner will certainly be found the President.

Office U. S. Military Telegraph,
WAR DEPARTMENT.

The following Telegram received at Washington, 9 15a M. Sept 6
21 from San Francisco Aug 26
via Denver 6th

The adjt Genl USA
Genl

President Juarez of the Republic
of Mexico & his Cabinet have been
forced by the French to leave Chihuahua
& are now in El Paso which is for the
present the seat of gov't of the Republic
How long Mr Juarez can remain at
that point with safety is doubtful, probably
not long I have offered him the
use of some fine dwellings at Hart's
Mills Franklin Texas should he be
forced to take refuge on our side
of the line.   Jas H Carleton

Transcript of a telegram received by the U.S. War Department from Brigadier General James H. Carleton, commander of the Department of New Mexico, concerning an offer of asylum to President Juárez—who declined with sincere thanks (*Courtesy of The National Archives*) (*Record Group 94, Adjutant General*) (*436–N–1865*)

By this time, the Americans' war of nerves was beginning to tell on the French. Bazaine had already been given secret orders not to go any nearer the border than Chihuahua (though Juárez did not know this). Napoleon now sent him instructions to consolidate defensively. This meant a French pull-out from many cities, principally in the north. The Juarists, naturally, moved in after them. Many Mexican imperialists redefected to the republic. Some of the Austrian and Belgian volunteers, long unpaid, did the same. The rank and file, in general, were accepted.

All this got Bazaine rattled. The Marshal complained that the Emperor's policy with deserters when caught was too lenient.

At the same time, word reached the capital that Juárez might soon cross into Texas. The message became garbled in transmission. Maximilian got it as "has crossed." On that erroneous basis, the Emperor, prodded by Bazaine, issued his infamous decree of October 3, 1865.

The decree began: "The cause sustained by don Benito Juárez with such valor has already succumbed . . . that cause has been left abandoned by the departure of its leader from the fatherland." These were the words of Maximilian. That which followed was dictated by others. All who continued to resist were outlaws. For those caught bearing arms against the Empire, no matter what the political pretext, the death penalty was mandatory—within twenty-four hours and without appeal. The decree was far severer than Juárez' of 1862, and it was more ruthlessly carried out. When Maximilian signed the decree of October 3, he signed his own death warrant.

Juárez' four-year term of office was to expire on December 1, 1865. If, at that time, elections could not be held, according to the constitution, the President of the Supreme Court should become president ad interim. This meant González Ortega. The victor of Calpulalpan had become an in-and-outer, and was suspected of flirting with the French. After his 1864 defeat in Durango, Ortega made great show of his determination to fight on, but noted that he might, in an emergency, need to cross the border to avoid capture. Juárez gave him a passport against such an emergency. Ortega promptly did cross the border and kept going till he hit New York. For over a year, in that city, he involved himself in all sorts of freewheeling, unauthorized dealings.

If Ortega returned, he might muster enough support to plunge the republic into civil war—a war within a war. After much pondering, Juárez made his decision. On November 8, acting under his extraordinary powers, he had Lerdo issue two decrees. The first extended the terms of both President and Chief Justice until the war should end and elections become possible. The second declared that Ortega had abandoned his office as chief justice, as well as his army commission, by remaining so long out of the country without permission.

As expected, there was an outcry: Juárez was attempting to perpetuate himself as dictator. He rode out the storm. His decision, politically, was soon vindicated. All his governors and all but two of his generals fell into line behind him.

Meanwhile, the peripatetic President almost got caught off base. On October 29, the French withdrew from Chihuahua. Juárez, apparently on faulty intelligence, decided to return there. Friendly Americans crossed the border to give him a farewell party, bringing with them a military band. There was dancing and card-playing. With a great to-do, the presidential party took off south. Then, the French started a drive back north toward Chihuahua. The little black carriage made a dignified but hasty trip back to the border.

This was to be its last retreat.

12

The Hill of the Bells

MAXIMILIAN'S TIME was running out. The American people and their government were getting more and more irritated by the French presence in Mexico. President Johnson and Secretary of State Seward grew more and more impatient with France's evasive answers to their diplomatic approaches. Johnson sent General Philip Sheridan to the border with a well-armed force of 100,000, as a warning to Maximilian and Bazaine. Large stocks of American arms, ammunition, and supplies were declared surplus, and ostentatiously left unguarded along the border. Each night that this was done, they were gone by morning.

On February 12, 1866, Seward issued a virtual ultimatum: it was clear that France was in Mexico against Mexico's will; the United States would be grateful to have from the French Emperor definite information as to when military operations might be expected to cease. The ultimatum was issued on the birthday of the man who had said: "When that army is gone, the Mexicans will take care of Maximilian."

In Mexico, Napoleon could see, Juárez and his government were dug in to stay—American aid or no American aid. In Europe, Bismarck's Prussia was a growing menace. Aside from the Mexican situation, Napoleon needed his troops at home. In

April, 1866, he decided to cut his losses and pull out. The army was to depart in three stages, the last troops to leave in November, 1867. When, in mid-1866, Prussia defeated Austria in a seven–week war, even that timetable was moved ahead.

Maximilian received warnings from Europe, but he still lived in a world apart. He calmly took the attitude that he was working for Mexico and would be only too happy to accept the collaboration of Juárez in that effort. Until Napoleon actually made his decision to withdraw, Maximilian continued to put full trust and credence in the promise that he would never be deserted. His awakening must have been a brutal one.

Miramón had made his way back from Europe. With Mejía and Márquez, Maximilian had three first-rate troop commanders. His non-French forces, including the Austrians and Belgians who had not deserted, numbered in the neighborhood of 10,000. Yet the republican generals were closing in. Even the tough and resourceful Mejía took a bad beating at the hands of a rising Juarist star, General Mariano Escobedo.

Maximilian was on the point of abdicating. Carlota talked him out of it. She would go to Europe and intercede with Napoleon herself. On July 9, 1866, she left. The parting was a painful one for Maximilian, but Mexico sang satirically, "Goodbye Mama Carlota. Goodbye, my tender love."

Carlota's mission was a tragic and pathetic failure. Napoleon, with troubles closer to home, could or would do nothing for her. She began to give way to paranoia. A glass of orange juice brought her by the Emperor's servant became poison. Napoleon was the devil and was trying to kill her. She went to Rome to plead with the Pope. Pius IX received her in regal style, but he had not forgiven Maximilian's nonsupport. When he refused to intercede with Napoleon, Carlota's sanity left her. She refused to budge from the Vatican. Her brother came from Belgium and led her away. She lived on until 1927, totally insane.

Maximilian, rocked first by Napoleon's desertion then by the

news of Carlota's breakdown, again prepared to abdicate.
Napoleon himself had advised it. Bazaine entreated him to do
so and to leave with the troops. Others, ministers and generals
with a vested interest in his staying, pleaded with him to
remain. He finally promised to stay, provided—and this was
pure Maximilian—that a "national assembly" wished him to.
This was managed, though it was not easy. The Emperor put
aside his butterfly collection and set about organizing his
defenses.

On February 5, 1867, Marshal Bazaine and the last of the
French garrison marched out of the capital. Maximilian,
watching them go from his palace window, is reported to have
said: "At last I am free." It was the freedom of despair, and
Maximilian must surely have known it.

Juárez and his ministers, backed up against the border,
directed operations to the extent that communications
permitted. Gradually, the going got better. The French were
out of the north. Porfirio Díaz and his brother Félix retook
Oaxaca. By the end of 1866, before the last French had left, only
Mexico City, Veracruz, and a few scattered areas elsewhere
remained under imperial control. The little black carriage
began its journey back, by slow stages.

Juárez, nonetheless, continued to push the law of averages.
In early 1867, Miramón, always audacious and offensive-
minded, made a lightning raid and took the city of Zacatecas in
mid-Mexico. In so doing, he gave the President, in that town on
his way south, one final cliff-hanger. Juárez commented: "If we
had delayed a quarter of an hour more in leaving the Palace, we
should have given a happy moment to Miramón, but we
escaped because the hour had not arrived."

For Maximilian, the hour had arrived. Once he had made the
agonizing decision to stick it out, his next move was to take the
field himself as commander-in-chief. Most of the imperial
forces were operating around Querétaro, some 125 miles north
of the capital. That city, a stronghold of religion and privilege,

Juárez' "little black carriage," reconstructed by order of President
Gustavo Díaz Ordaz, which stands in the Museum of National
History in Chapultepec

was one of the few remaining provincial pockets of imperial
resistance. Maximilian decided to make his stand there. The die
was cast.

He had 9,000 men. The republicans under Escobedo had
three armies totaling 27,000. They were slow in converging,
however. The city was at first only lightly invested. While his
generals argued strategy and tactics, the Emperor wandered
about the front lines, exposing himself to enemy fire in order to
inspire his troops. From this time on, it appears, it was
Maximilian of Habsburg who was inspired. Gone at last was the
self-delusion, gone the sheltered innocence. The Emperor of
Mexico was through, he knew it, and he was resolved to finish
things off in style and good taste.

On February 21, 1867, Benito Juárez arrived in San Luis
Potosí and unfurled his flag. His first stop on the long journey

that started from the capital in 1863 was now his last stop before the capital on the way back. Before he left the border, he had approved Pedro Santacilia's plan for bringing his family back to Veracruz by ship, once the enemy had given up the port.

Aside from the tragedy of her two sons, doña Margarita was getting along reasonably well in New York—often with one of her daughters as English interpreter. When she visited Romero at the legation in Washington, and the White House found out about it, she was invited to a presidential reception and made much of. She wrote Juárez that it was there, for the first time, that she wore the dress he had bought as her going-away present in Monterrey. ("I tell you all this because they shall not say that when you were in El Paso in such poverty I was here enjoying luxury.")

There was also a dinner given by Secretary Seward, and a ball given by General Grant. ("He was very kind.") Yet Margarita, her grief still fresh within her, was only going through the motions. Although her letters to Juárez were full of common sense and tart disapproval of the risks he took, one passage completely revealed her heart: "I shall have peace only when at last I am with you."

By March 6, Escobedo's forces had surrounded Querétaro and started cutting off food and water. There were still sorties, however, and occasional skirmishes. One night, Márquez and Vidaurri, at Maximilian's order, escaped with 1,200 cavalry. They were to go to Mexico City and return with reinforcements—as well as books and wine for Maximilian. Márquez increased his force to 4,000 in the capital, but had no desire to bottle himself up. He set out for Puebla, where he was met and defeated by Porfirio Díaz. Márquez himself escaped, as usual.

Getting news of this grave setback to their hopes, the stay-behinds in Querétaro decided to throw everything into one last attempt to break through. On the eve of their attempt, they were betrayed. A Colonel Miguel López, to whose child

Maximilian had stood godfather, secretly let the republicans in at night and guided them to Maximilian's headquarters. In the scuffle that followed, Miramón was wounded. Maximilian was given his last unofficial chance to escape, but did not take it. (There had been others; the Emperor had consistently refused to desert his side.) With Tomás Mejía, he made his way to the little *Cerro de las Campanas* (Hill of the Bells), just outside town. There, on May 15, 1867, they were surrounded and forced to surrender.

Juárez ordered Maximilian, Miramón, and Mejía court-martialed in accordance with his decree of January 25, 1862 (death for foreigners conspiring against Mexican independence and for Mexicans aiding them). The trial began on June 12. Maximilian refused to attend but was given good lawyers. Their chief defense was that he had become a Mexican partisan chieftain. The prosecution's big gun was Maximilian's decree of October 3, 1865. It had led to the death of many Mexicans, as had his carrying on the war after the French had left. Three of the court-martial officers voted for banishment, four for death. The death verdict included Miramón and Mejía.

The world was agog. Royalty and diplomats made representations. Secretary Seward added his voice to the pleas for clemency. Impassioned appeals for mercy were telegraphed by Giuseppe Garibaldi and Victor Hugo, both staunch friends of Juárez' cause. On the other hand, many European liberals rejoiced—among them Georges Clemenceau (quoted earlier). In the eye of the storm, outwardly calm and imperturbable, sat Benito Juárez.

In Querétaro itself, various plots were afoot for Maximilian's escape. The Emperor refused to go along with these lest he sully his honor. Finally, he did consent to an escape scheme that involved bribing his guards, and he signed several large checks payable by the imperial family of Austria. The scheme was the brain child of the Prince and Princess Salm-Salm, a colorful pair. He was a German soldier of fortune of noble birth, had served in the Union army, then had attached himself to Maximilian—whose captivity he now shared.

Agnes Joy Salm-Salm, American-born and a one-time circus rider, was, evidently, quite a woman. In her memoirs, she tells how she tried to bribe the Colonel of the guard with Maximilian's check for $100,000, "if he would only consent to turn his back and close his eyes for ten minutes." She conjectures that the Colonel, an Indian, may not have known what a check was. In any case, he refused and reported her to General Escobedo. Escobedo, who had let her into Querétaro to see her husband, was furious. He ordered her sent to San Luis Potosí, under guard. There, he said, she could make her plea to the President. At the same time, he expelled the many foreign diplomats who had gathered in Querétaro to consult and conspire.

In San Luis, the Princess, who had seen Juárez before, was granted an interview. The President knew all about the attempted bribery, and, according to her account, gave the clear impression that the escape of the Emperor would by no means "have been very disagreeable to him."

Maximilian, ever quixotic, telegraphed Juárez to intercede for Miramón and Mejía, that he might be the only one to die. Many personages, diplomats and highborn ladies—including Miramón's wife and child—besieged the presidential offices in San Luis. But it could not be. Even Benito Juárez, least vengeful of men, could not put personal considerations above justice and the national interest. Perhaps he wished that Maximilian had escaped—but Maximilian had not.

The night before the execution, the Princess Salm-Salm made a final effort with Juárez. She recounts:

It was eight o'clock in the evening when I went to see M. Juárez, who received me at once. He looked pale and suffering himself. With trembling lips I pleaded for the life of the Emperor, or at least for delay. The president said he could not grant it; he would not prolong his agony any longer; the Emperor must die tomorrow.

When I heard these cruel words I became frantic with grief. Trembling in every limb and sobbing, I fell down on my knees, and pleaded with words which came from my heart, but which I cannot remember. The president tried to raise me, but I held his knees convulsively, and would not leave him before he had granted his life. I saw the president was moved; he as well as M. Iglesia had tears in their eyes, but he answered with a low, sad voice, "I am grieved, madam, to see you thus on your knees before me; but if all the kings and queens of Europe were in your place I could not spare that life. It is not I who takes it, it is the people and the law; and if I should not do its will, the people would take it and mine also.

On June 19, 1867, the execution took place, on that same *Cerro de las Campanas* where Maximilian had surrendered. The day was sunny as Maximilian, Miramón, and Mejía were brought from their carriages and stood against the wall. Maximilian, chivalrous to the end, ceded the central place of honor to Miramón, in tribute to a good soldier. When the captain of the firing squad asked forgiveness, Maximilian smiled, thanked the officer, and bade him to do his duty. In a final brief statement, he said: "May my blood put an end to the misfortunes of my new country." The volley rang out. As Maximilian of Habsburg fell to the ground, he muttered *"hombre!"*—then was given the *coup de grâce*.

The world uproar continued for some time. Juárez was berated in much of the world press. Censure and sympathy, however, often were related to class feeling. Not all comment was abusive. The French workers saluted him as one of their own. The sentimental appeal of Maximilian, the charmer, revolted many of Europe's intellectual left.

Juárez himself rested his case on the judgment of posterity. That judgment, though mellowed with time, has never given him a full pardon. Yet he did what he had to do, unflinchingly, as was the Juárez way. In a manifesto dated July 17 he noted that, aside from theory and international law, Mexico had its own law—that of January 25, 1862—enacted to punish piratical invasion. He concluded:

> The penalty that Maximilian suffered was just, because it balanced an unspeakable crime. . . . The example of the penal sanction has been necessary for the European monarchs. Theoretical or moral persuasion is futile against them, but our penal law will reveal to them for the future the hazards and immorality of their so-called interventions in America.

As Juárez had said many years before, the law was his sword and his shield.

While Maximilian was being executed, Porfirio Díaz had the capital under siege. On June 21, the garrison surrendered unconditionally. Márquez, slippery to the end, managed to disappear in the confusion. He made it to Havana, where he ended his days as an obscure pawnbroker. Vidaurri was shot trying to escape. A few other leaders were killed, but most were banished, fined, or pardoned. The foreign troops were allowed to make their way back to Europe.

On July 3, Juárez left San Luis Potosí. He arrived in Chapultepec, at the edge of the capital, on July 13. Díaz, who had managed his collections and confiscations as well as his battles, was able to turn over a considerable sum to the government. (A bit of this he blew on a triumphal homecoming for Benito Juárez.) On July 15, the little black carriage entered the city, a small and sober centerpiece to the garlands of flowers, flags, and welcome messages. The latter, whether on banners, placards, or arches, bore a simple message from the heart: The People to Juárez.

Porfirio Díaz had not forgotten that day in 1863, when the red, white, and green tricolor had been lowered at sunset and given into the care of a President taking off into God knew what future. He had had a large, new flag made, and had given strict orders that no colors should be raised on the National Palace flagstaff. As the President drove up through the massed troops, Díaz, at stiff attention, presented the new flag to his chief. Juárez himself ran it up the staff. As in 1863, he cried: *"Viva México!"* The crowd roared it back—this time with joy.

The President's message to his people was simple and moving. He thanked the good sons of Mexico who, alone, had saved the republic; he promised to temper justice toward former enemies with all possible mercy; and, again, he swore to uphold the constitution and the laws. "The people and the government shall respect the rights of all. Between individuals as between nations, respect for the rights of others is peace."

One thing Juárez still lacked, and that was soon forthcoming. Through the courtesy of the United States Government, the revenue cutter *Wilderness* was put at the disposal of "Madame Juárez and party, fourteen persons in all." On July 14, 1867, the cutter docked at Veracruz—and the rejoicing was not for Bastille Day. On July 25, the homing party reached Mexico City. With tragic gaps in the ranks, the family of Benito and Margarita Juárez was together again at last.

13

The Last Years

MEXICO HAD the foundations of true nationhood at last. Would that the Juárez story could have ended here, with everyone living happily ever after. Alas, it could not be. The President's final five years were to bring little but pain and trouble. Not the crisis-type, operational trouble that Juárez was used to and took in stride, but a whole postwar syndrome of frustration, disillusionment, and gnawing restlessness.

After fifty-seven years of struggle, ending with almost a decade of shooting war, the nation was exhausted. Although the invader had been thrown out, he paid no reparations. The treasury was all but empty. The economy, still primitive, remained stubbornly stagnant. The people were still backward and largely illiterate. The army had to be reduced drastically, and few of the discharged could be adequately recompensed. Many of them had known no life but war, and quite a number took to banditry. The political opposition, though numerically small, gained important recruits from the disaffected among Juárez' own following, and they became increasingly articulate. On top of the general malaise came the death of Margarita, a shattering blow to her devoted spouse. Yet Juárez held on. It was all he knew how to do.

Almost as soon as hostilities had ceased, the man who had

made his mark as governor of Oaxaca turned his hand, once again, to the constructive, the concrete. He set in motion an intensive program of road-building and vigorously reactivated construction of the Mexico City–Veracruz railroad—for which he managed to obtain some British capital. Most importantly, as in the Oaxaca days, Juárez put his energies to building up a viable national school system. In so doing, he actually ran ahead of France and England in introducing the three essential features of modern schooling. Elementary education was made compulsory, gratis, and free of religious instruction.

It was taken for granted that Juárez would run again for president in 1867. Although many politicians and generals were tired of him, the people were not. They owed him a debt of honor, and they wanted to pay it.

Juárez was opposed by Sebastián Lerdo de Tejada, still acting as his chief minister, and by Porfirio Díaz, idol of the veterans and chosen instrument of the opposition. Relations between the President and his top general had been cooling since the triumphal entry into the capital. Juárez could not seem to realize that "our Porfirio" had grown up, that the ex-pupil and daring junior officer was now an energetic and ambitious leader in his forties. Díaz had strong and potentially dangerous support among the disillusioned veteran element. He was urged and tempted to seize power then and there, but decided to play it straight.

Juárez won re-election by a landslide. Lerdo, a poor second, won the number two spot of chief justice and vice president. Díaz retired to his estate in Oaxaca and bided his time.

In issuing the call for the 1867 elections, Juárez had made a grave tactical error. In addition to presidential and congressional balloting, he called for voting on a series of constitutional amendments that were designed mainly to strengthen the executive vis-à-vis the congress. The amendments were largely Lerdo's idea, but Juárez stood behind them.

The outcry was loud and immediate. Dictatorship! The

opposition was led by Manuel Zamacona, who had been Juárez' foreign minister during the first days of the British-French-Spanish intervention. He threw everything but the kitchen sink against the amendments. In the end, the government gave up, and did not even count the votes on the issue. Even so, it lost considerable face. The opposition, thwarted in its choice for president, took to name-calling and character assassination as standard operational procedure.

In January, 1868, Juárez recalled the faithful Matías Romero from Washington and handed him the hot potato of the Treasury. Romero labored valiantly to re-establish fiscal order and get on with reconstruction. He started two new railway projects and made a beginning at reviving mining and agriculture. He tried, also, to do away with bureaucratic barriers to the attraction of foreign capital but was stymied by a vindictive and well-organized opposition. In any case, brigandage was by now a serious factor, and it discouraged foreign investors.

In foreign affairs, Juárez took the position that it was up to the European powers—those that had recognized Maximilian—to take the initiative. If they wanted to renew relations, it must be on Mexico's terms—and with no fancy ideas about residual financial claims. Relations with the United States were cordial. A mixed claims commission cleared up outstanding claims of both sides, dating back to 1848. With Washington as go-between, relations were resumed with Italy and the German Confederation. In 1869, to Juárez' delight, Mexico's friend General Prim overthrew the Spanish Queen, established a constitutional monarchy, and asked to renew relations.

In 1870, Bismarck tricked Napoleon, by then a very sick man, into a war he was ill prepared to fight. (Napoleon's Mexican blunder had seen to that.) The Emperor ended up in exile. As for Marshal Bazaine, he disgraced himself at the defense of Metz. According to France's leading encyclopedia, he let himself be boxed into the town, made only "derisory" efforts to extricate himself, entered into some very questionable negotiations with Bismarck, then surrendered the city. He was sentenced to death in 1873. When this was commuted to life imprisonment, he escaped and ended his days in Spain.

The downfall of Napoleon could not help but cast reflected glory on Juárez. Mexico's pride in him was reawakened. The world was reminded of how the Indian David had bested the French Goliath—and, in so doing, softened him up for another's kill. In due course, the new French republic itself was duly grateful. To Benito Juárez, who was only human, recognition must have been sweet.

Things were not at all well with the Juárez family, however. Doña Margarita fell prey to a long and painful illness. In October, 1870, the President himself suffered a form of stroke. For some days, it was touch and go. Only the iron Juárez

Porfirio Díaz
at age forty-six

Sebastián Lerdo de Tejada

constitution pulled him through. No sooner had he got back on his feet than he was sent reeling by the heaviest blow of all. On January 2, 1871, Margarita Maza de Juárez died.

There would never be another quite like her. Whether trekking across forbidding mountains to join her husband in Veracruz or receiving honors in Washington's White House, Margarita Juárez had typified the very best in Mexican womanhood. Devoted wife, mother, and patriot, she had taken the rough with the smooth for the twenty-seven years of their life together—a union of heart and mind the like of which has seldom been seen. Margarita was forty-four years old when she died. Seven of her twelve children survived her.

A truce was called to polemics. The opposition leaned over backward. A scathing editorial against Juárez was pulled out of the press and replaced with a tribute to Margarita that could be nothing but sincere. Two ringleaders of recent uprisings, pardoned by Juárez, were among the pallbearers. Mexico and the world mourned with the widower. A leading paper wrote: "We have never seen a similar unanimity of feelings or an equal expression of sorrow among all classes of the population, without regard to party, opinion, or nationality."

It was the best part of a month before the President could get focused on his work. Meanwhile, the elections of 1871 were drawing close. Perhaps in spite of his wife's death, perhaps because of it, Benito Juárez refused to retire. He announced his candidacy for re-election.

It has been said that Lincoln died in time, while Juárez outlived his mission. He certainly did not quit while he was ahead. Inevitably, the accusations of dictatorial ambitions renewed and multiplied. There was talk of His Majesty Benito I. Malicious parodies went the rounds. Yet, it does not seem that Juárez was attached to power so much as he was attached to his job—to the life of crisis, decision, and responsibility that had been his since the night he gave Zuloaga the slip in 1858. He just did not know how to quit. If he believed himself indispensable, he was not the first in history to think so—nor the last.

In the electoral campaign, Juárez gave the press complete freedom. That freedom was used with a vengeance, but the President put his faith in the country's common sense. As in 1867, he was opposed by Lerdo and Díaz. Lerdo's support was largely upper crust, though not necessarily "conservative." (There were only "liberals" now.) Díaz' backing took in a wide range of men, whose common denominator was discontent. The platforms of the contenders differed only in emphasis and degree.

The electoral votes cast for Juárez fell 5 per cent short of an absolute majority. Again, the election was thrown into congress. On October 8, the lawmakers gave Juárez a surprising 108 votes, with only 5 for Lerdo and 3 for Díaz.

Before and during the elections, there had been a series of armed uprisings, starting in the north and spreading through the country. A few days before congress made Juárez' election official, a garrison mutinied in the capital itself. The Minister of War being away, the President showed some of his old *sang-froid* by taking command in person to break it up. Something more serious was yet in store, however.

When congress confirmed his defeat at the polls, Porfirio Díaz—not unexpectedly—went on the warpath himself. His brother Félix, Governor of Oaxaca, had for some time been stockpiling arms and ammunition brought in by sea from New York. The Díazes commanded 3,500 well-armed men and the loyalty of the Oaxaca state congress. On November 8, 1871, Porfirio published his Plan of Noria, named for the Oaxaca estate given him by the government. Principally, it called for a new constitutional convention and for a "provisional president" who was inescapably intended to be the author of the plan. While pretending to sustain the constitution, it, in effect, set that charter aside and called for a military dictatorship.

Díaz had misread Mexico's state of mind. Contrary to what he had obviously expected, the nation gave him a resounding "No!" No more revolutions, no more military pronouncements! The political opposition, for once, lined up with Juárez. The people were right behind them. The government broke up the insurrection in a brief campaign. Félix Díaz got shot. Porfirio Díaz took to the hills.

Once this threat to the peace was removed, the warriors of the opposition returned to the charge. Juárez was once more subjected to an unceasing crossfire of carping, nitpicking, and general sniping. By now the President was quite above it all. He simply ignored the slings and arrows and went about the business of governing. As for Díaz, he lay low and bided his time. It would come soon enough.

Benito Juárez was very much alone. His daughters took good care of him, and he loved them, but they were not Margarita. In the fifty-three years since the shepherd boy had left home and walked to the big city, how many had come and gone—the good ones and the bad! And how few had died in bed! Had Juárez been a gambling man, he might have amused himself calculating the odds he had beaten by just surviving. Confrontation after confrontation, cliff-hanger after cliff-hanger, all faced up to with the detached matter-of-factness of the true fatalist.

One faithful friend remained—the people. They still loved him, and they always would. "The People to Juárez." The aging President often strolled the streets, sometimes with a companion but frequently alone—or with a security man a discreet few paces behind. On his walks, he was free. Free to let his gaze linger on the playing children—the Mexico of the future. Free to smile at ordinary men and women, and often be smiled at in return. Shopkeepers and artisans, farmers bringing in their produce, wood carriers arguing with their burros, little ladies selling everything from edible cactus to lottery numbers. These were what mattered—not the everlasting generals and politicians.

When death beckoned, Juárez was not unprepared. In the spring of 1872, he had two brief heart attacks. The second came while he was playing host to a group of orphans at the Palace. He paled and leaned for a moment on a table, but never let the children notice.

On July 18, 1872, the President's physician was summoned urgently. Juárez was in the throes of angina pectoris—a heart seizure. The treatment in those days was to pour scalding water over the heart—a heroic remedy but one that did stimulate the organ into going on, for a while at least. Between each bout and its excruciating remedy, there was a respite of several hours. During those hours, the President carried on business as usual. That night, he seemed so much better that the family left his side and went in to dinner.

Left with the doctor, the sick man rambled about his

boyhood, especially about don Antonio Salanueva. Suddenly, he threw in a question: "Doctor, is my illness mortal?" The physician could not lie to Benito Juárez. He said gently that it was. His patient took the answer in stride and went on conversing.

More attacks followed. The people knew the President was ill, but not how ill. The Foreign Minister, thinking it was rheumatism, insisted on seeing his chief to get some guidance. After he had left, a general came for the same purpose. Both found Juárez sitting up, wrapped in a shawl, and both got the advice they wanted. Neither noticed anything out of the ordinary.

No one saw the stoic little Indian die. The faithful physician, though he never left his patient's side, had dozed off unwittingly and was asleep at the fatal moment. When he awoke with a start, a bit before midnight, Benito Juárez had quietly passed into immortality.

Next morning, all Mexico heard the news. The world heard it soon thereafter. All pettiness was put aside. As the cannon thundered, tribute was paid without stint—tribute to the man who had become the very incarnation of a cause, the standard-bearer of the republic, the holder of the passes against the invader. Through streets lined with massed and muted mourners, a simple coffin, unadorned and unpretentious, was carried to its last resting place.

Benito Juárez was with his Margarita. His death mask, preserved for posterity, shows no sign of storm or stress—only a faint, peaceful smile.

14

Epilogue

THE NOTED Mexican writer Andrés Iduarte has said: "Benito Juárez is Mexico and Mexico is Juárez." Juárez personifies, as no other man, the values that unite all Mexicans—even those few who still do not love him. His people, today, look upon him as the builder of modern Mexico. The country's first statute to establish the equality of all men under the law bears his name. By winning the long and bitter fight against foreign interference, he affirmed for all time the sovereign right of Mexico to decide its own destiny.

Juárez and the reform destroyed Mexican feudalism and brought a new middle class—much of it mestizo, some of it Indian—into the national life. Ironically for Juárez the Zapotec, the reform was not able markedly to integrate the pure Indian peasant into the Mexican mainstream. Mexico, today, still strives toward that goal. Yet, it is only at the end of the Juárez period that one may properly begin to speak of a Mexican nation in the present-day sense.

Juárez left much undone. His work endures because, although unfinished, it was progress. Progress has no end. The true heroes of history contribute to it, and, contributing, themselves become part of its never ending course.

At the turn of the century, the cantankerous Francisco

Búlnes rose against the established, comfortably mummified Juárez cult. Búlnes rekindled the controversies of 1871–72. His arguments were so patently slanted and his bias so obvious that his fabrications were easily shown up for what they were. Yet the exercise served a purpose. In the furor of controversy that followed, Juárez the national hero was vindicated but the limitations of Juárez the man were acknowledged. Along with the many strengths, some weaknesses were recognized. Benito Juárez was human after all. The saint, decanonized, was taken down from his unneeded pedestal and made man again.

Juárez was no a superman, nor was he an intellectual giant. His genius lay in evoking, and using to his beloved Mexico's best advantage, the energies and intellectual brilliance of others. He was their goad and their conscience. Cool courage, bulldog tenacity, unquestioned integrity, total commitment—these combined to produce a moral force that friend could not but emulate and foe could not ignore.

The role of Juárez as Mexico's man of destiny has been admirably summed up by a respected Mexican historian, Justo Sierra, who wrote:

> It is not the pure philosophers—no matter how elevated or transcendental their thoughts—who are called upon to personify these vertiginous moments of social evolution; it is the men whose supreme quality is character, an unbreakable will. Without men like Lerdo, Ocampo, and Ramírez, revolutions are not possible; without men like Juárez, they are not accomplished.

Benito Juárez is Mexico. Mexico is Benito Juárez.

Principal Dates in the Life of Juárez

1806.   Born at San Pablo Guelatao.

1810.   *Hidalgo's uprising.*

1811–15.   *Morelos' uprising.*

1818.   Leaves home for Oaxaca.

1821.   Enters Holy Cross Seminary.
            Mexican independence from Spain.

1824.   *First Mexican constitution.*

1828.   Enters Institute of Arts and Science.

1831.   Elected alderman.

1833.   Elected to state legislature.
            First presidency of Santa Anna.

1834.   Admitted to bar.
            Episode at Loxicha.

1841.   Appointed judge.

1843.   Marries Margarita Maza.

1845.   Seated on state supreme court

1846.   Elected to national congress, goes to Mexico
             City.
             United States invades Mexico.

1847–52.   Governor of Oaxaca.

1853–55.   Deported by Santa Anna. Exile in New
             Orleans.

1855.   Minister of Justice and Public Instruction in
             reform government.
             Publication of *Ley Juárez.*

1856.   Governor of Oaxaca.
             Publication of *Ley Tejada.*

1857.   Minister of Interior and Chief Justice (Vice
             President).
             Second Mexican Constitution.
             Arrested by Zuloaga after conservative coup.

1858.   Escapes from capital, sworn in as President by
             state governors.
             Civil war begins.
             After several moves, establishes government at
             Veracruz.

1859.   Publication of reform laws.

1860.   *Conservative army surrenders.*

1861.   Re-enters capital.
             Returned to presidency through elections.
             U. S. Civil War begins.

1862.   *French-British-Spanish intervention. British
             and Spanish pull out.
             French, defeated at Puebla, return to base.*

1863.   With French menacing capital, moves
             government to Sån Luis Potosí.

1864.   Moves government successively to Saltillo,
             Monterrey, Chihuahua.
             Maximilian and Carlota arrive in Vera Cruz.

1865.   Moves government to El Paso del Norte on
             Texas border.
             Lee surrenders at Appomattox.
             Extends term of office by decree, for the
             duration.

1866.   With French phase-out started, begins slow
             trek back from border.
             Carlota departs for Europe.

1867.   Re-establishes government at San Luis Potosí.
             Last French troops leave Mexico.
             Maximilian surrenders and is executed.
             Returns in triumph to capital. Re-elected
             President.

1871.   Runs again for presidency despite wife's death.
             Re-elected.
             Dies.

Suggestions for Further Reading

HOWARD F. CLINE, *The United States and Mexico* (New York: Athenaeum, 1963; paperback reprint).

RALPH ROEDER, *Juarez and His Mexico* (New York: Greenwood Press, 1968).

WALTER V. SCHOLES, *Mexican Politics During the Juárez Regime, 1855-1872* (Columbia: University of Missouri Studies, 30, 1957).

CHARLES ALLEN SMART, *Viva Juárez!* (Philadelphia and New York: J. B. Lippincott Company, 1963).

Index